गीतासार

Kashmiri Gītāsāra

गीतासार

Kashmiri Gītāsāra

The Issue of the Bhagavadgītā
with 745 Verses

Devanāgarī with Transliteration
and English Translation

Gerard D. C. Kuiken

Also by the Author

Thermodynamics of Irreversible Processes, John Wiley, 1994
Eastern Thought and the Gita, OTAM Books, 2012
The Original Gita: Striving for Oneness, Motilal Banarsidass, 2012, 2015
The Shiva Sutra of Vasugupta, OTAM Books, 2017, 2023
The Roots of the Bhagavadgītā, Volumes I, II, III, OTAM Books, 2023

Kashmiri Gītāsāra: The Issue of the Bhagavadgītā with 745 *Verses*

Publisher: OTAM Books
Website: www.gdckuiken.com
Email: g.d.c.kuiken@planet.nl for comments and corrections

ISBN 978-90-78623-15-1

Cover design: Margaret Kay Dodd, Studio K Arts, USA
Email: studiokarts@earthlink.net

Printed in the USA

Contents

Abbreviations

abl., ablative case
abs., absolutive
acc., accusative case
act., active voice, parasmaipada
adj., adjective, see mfn.
adv., adverb
BG, *BhG*, BG, *Bhagavadgītā*
caus., causative
cpd, compound
dat., dative case
du., dual
esp., especially
f., feminine gender
fpp., future passive participle
gen., genitive case
imperf., imperfect tense
imperv., imperative mood
ibc., in the beginning of a cpd
i.e., id est: in other words
ifc., in fini compositi or "at the end of a compound"
ind., indeclinable
indic., indicative mood
inst., instrumental case
lit., literally
loc., locative case
m., masculine gender
mfn., masculine, female, neuter or = adjective
mid., middle voice, ātmanepada
n., neuter gender
nom., nominative case
opt., optative mood
partc., participle
pass., passive voice
perf., perfect tense
pers., personal
pl., plural
ppp., perfect passive participle
pr., present tense
pron., pronoun
sg., singular
voc., vocative case
1st, first person
2nd, second person
3rd, third person
√, verb root
- , prefix or suffix hyphen
°, abbreviation symbol

Introductory remarks

The *Bhagavadgītā* (*BhG*) is one of the best known of all the Indian spiritual scriptures. Dating and authorship of the *BhG* have been discussed by the author elsewhere.[1]

The *BhG* is divided into 18 chapters, and Śaṃkara (788–820 CE) declared in the beginning of his *Gītābhāṣya* (Commentary on the *BhG*) that it contains 700 verses.[2] The 700 verses are also the number of verses found in the Critical Edition of the *BhG*.[3] However, some manuscripts in the Critical Apparatus have extra verses, found in the footnotes of the Critical Edition, and marked as "star-passages." A number[4] of Kashmirian recensions of the *Mahābhārata* (*MBh*) have inserted after the *BhG* a verse known as the *Gītāmāna* or the extent of the *BhG*,[5] declaring that the *BhG* has 745 verses. It specified that Krishna spoke 620 verses, Arjuna 57, Sanjaya 67, and Dhritarashtra one. In these Kashmirian recensions, the *Gītāmāna* is followed by 51 verses, known as the *Gītāsāra*,[6] the quintessence or the summary of the *BhG*. Belvalkar[7] has argued that the enhanced extent of the *BhG* is the extent of the *BhG* with the *Gītāsāra*. Compared to the *Gītāmāna*, this total has 6 verses too many; also Krishna spoke 2 and Arjuna 30 verses too many, while Sanjaya is short by 26 verses.[8]

Belvalkar[9] found that the total is reduced by four verses when transforming three 4-line verses into two 6-line verses, of which there

---

1 Kuiken 2018, reprint 2023, Vol. II, pp. 3–39; Kuiken 2016.

2 "*gītākhyaiḥ saptabhiḥ ślokaśataiḥ.*" Of these, 645 are *śloka* verses having 4 lines of 8 syllables, and 55 are *triṣṭubh* verses having 4 lines of 11 syllables. The warrior Arjuna spoke 84 verses; his charioteer and teacher Krishna 574 verses; Sanjaya, the narrator and charioteer of the blind King Dhritarashtra, 41 verses; and the king, 1 verse.

3 Belvalkar 1968, pp. 2–77.

4 Belvalkar 1968, p. xv; Bagchee and Adluri 2016, pp. 2, 14, 21, 23.

5 Belvalkar 1939, p. 336; Belvalkar 1968, p. 77, passage 112*; Saha 2018, pp. 148–150.

6 *Gītāsāra*: Krishna 48 + Arjuna 3 = 51. Belvalkar 1968, pp. 79–82, Appendix I, No. 3.

7 Belvalkar 1939; also Rastogi, 1975, pp. 37–38.

8 Krishna 622 + Arjuna 87 + Sanjaya 41 + Dhritarashtra 1 = 751.

9 Belvalkar 1939, pp. 344–47.

are 4,289 in the *MBh*,[10] bringing the total to 747 verses. Belvalkar mentioned that many words of Arjuna and Krishna are not their direct words but paraphrases by Sanjaya of their words. The verses BG1.21cd–23 and BG1.28cd–46 can be considered as paraphrasing Arjuna by Sanjaya, which reduces Arjuna's verses and increases Sanjaya's verses by 21. Omitting *Śrībhagavān uvāca* from BG2.2–3 and *Arjuna uvāca* from BG2.4–8 increases Sanjaya's verses by 7, reduces Krishna's verses by 2, and Arjuna's verses by 5.[11] Belvalkar found in the whole of the *BhG* not more than eight possibilities to form 6-line verses for Sanjaya and Arjuna, reducing each of their number of verses by 2. The four 6-line verses, BG1.20–21ab, BG1.21cd–22, and BG1.26–27ab, BG1.29cd–30, obtain for Sanjaya 67 verses, and BG10.13–14ab, BG10.14cd–15, and BG11.36–37ab with BG11.39cd–40 reduce Arjuna's spoken verses by 2. Arjuna still has an excess of two verses.[12] Except for omitting the introductions of two speakers, the words in the *BhG* have not been changed or reduced. Two verses spoken by Arjuna had to be omitted from the *BhG* to conform with the number of verses mentioned for Arjuna in the *Gītāmāna*. In his 1939 paper, Belvalkar referred to the Garbe-Otto[13] expedient of dropping the two verses BG8.1–2, in which Arjuna asked eight questions, to comply with the number of verses spoken by each speaker given in the *Gītāmāna*. However, in 1968, Belvalkar did not adopt the Garbe-Otto expedient of dropping BG8.1–2 anymore, as he stated in the "Editorial Note" to the Critical Edition of the *BhG* on page xxiv that "There remains at the end of the operation a small inevitable error of just 2 extra stanzas for Arjuna which cannot be eliminated."

The Kashmir recension has an introductory verse to Chapter 13 (not found in the Calcutta edition of the *MBh*) in which Arjuna expressed his wish to understand the following six basic concepts: Primordial Substance (*prakṛti*); Primordial Spirit (*puruṣa*); the field (*kṣetra*);

---

[10] The number of 6-line *ślokas* in the *Mahābhārata* is 4,177, and of 6-line *triṣṭubhs* is 112. Kuiken 2018, reprint 2023, Vol. II, p. 26.

[11] Krishna 620 + Arjuna 61 + Sanjaya 69 + Dhritarashtra 1 = 751.

[12] Krishna 620 + Arjuna 59 + Sanjaya 67 + Dhritarashtra 1 = 747.

[13] Belvalkar 1939, p. 347; Kuiken 2018, reprint 2023, Vol. II, p. 29.

the knower of the field (*kṣetrajña*); knowledge (*jñāna*); and the to-be-known (*jñeya*). This verse is not a part of the Critical Edition of the *BhG*, but it is given in "star-passage" 108*. Belvalkar[14] suggested that it was added only to lessen the abruptness of the introduction of the "field and the knower of the field (*kṣetra–kṣetrajña*)." The answers are given in Chapter 13, and indeed, in the answer the question is implied. The abruptness of *kṣetra* and *kṣetrajña* is questionable, since *kṣetrajña* occurs 12 times and *kṣetra* 84 times before their occurrence in verse BG13.1 of the *BhG* in the *MBh*, contrary to the occurrence of the *adhi*° words introduced in BG7.30.

An analogue situation holds for BG8.1–2, which is included in the Critical Edition, lessening the abruptness of the introduction of the "essence of elements" (*adhibhūta*), the "essence of the divine agent" (*adhidaiva*), and the "essence of sacrifice" (*adhiyajña*) in BG7.30, the last verse of Chapter 7. Of these three concepts, only *adhiyajña* has occurred before BG7.30 once in the *MBh* (MB2.30.29a). By their introduction in BG7.30, their occurrence in 8.1–2 might be considered as being redundant, as the questions are implied in the answers given in BG8.3–5. The concept of *adhyātman* occurs 14 times in the *MBh* before the *BhG*, and *brahman, action* and *knowing Krishna* have occurred many times before BG8.1–2. As such, BG8.1–2 might be qualified as a "star-passage" for the Kashmir recension of the extended *BhG*, thus agreeing fully with the specifications given in the *Gītāmāna*.

Bhattacharjya[15] deleted in his book, *The Original Bhagavad Gita Complete with 745 Verses (including all the Rare Verses)*, the verse BG11.46, and without discussion the two half-verses BG1.27ab and BG1.37cd. He added 46 verses from various sources, and attributed them to Krishna to comply with the *Gītāmāna*. Agreeing with Bhattacharjya that verse BG11.46 is a late interpolation that should have been inserted before verse BG11.45, only one of the verses BG8.1–2 has to be assigned a star-passage in the Kashmiri extended *BhG* to fulfill the *Gītāmāna*. By choosing BG8.2, the reference to *adhyātman* remains.

14 Belvalkar 1968, p. 54, and critical note on p. 104.

15 Bhattacharjya 2014, p. 32; Kuiken 2023, Vol. II, pp. 35–36; Vol. III, p. 124; Bedekar 1964.

Gītāmāna

ṣaṭ śatāni saviṃśāni
ślokānāṃ prāha keśavaḥ |
arjunaḥ saptapañcāśat
saptaṣaṣṭis tu saṃjayaḥ |
dhṛtarāṣṭraḥ ślokam ekaṃ
gītāyā mānam ucyate ||

षट्शतानि सविंशानि
श्लोकानां प्राह केशवः ।
अर्जुनः सप्तपञ्चाशत्
सप्तषष्टिस्तु संजयः ।
धृतराष्ट्रः श्लोकमेकं
गीताया मानमुच्यते ॥

षट् ṣaṭ [ind.] *six times* शतानि śatāni [n. acc. pl. śata] *hundreds* सविंशानि saviṃśāni [n. acc. pl. sa-viṃśa] *and twenty* श्लोकानाम् ślokānām [m. gen. pl. śloka] *of verses, of praising or hymning in verses* प्राह prāha [3rd sg. perf. indic. act. prāh] *spoke, said, expressed, declared* केशवः keśavaḥ [m. nom. sg. keśava] *having long or much or handsome hair, an epithet of Viṣṇu or Kṛṣṇa* अर्जुनः arjunaḥ [m. nom. sg. arjuna] *Arjuna* सप्त sapta [f. number] *seven* पञ्चाशत् pañcāśat [f. nom. sg. pañcāśat] *fifty* सप्त sapta [f. cardinal number] *seven* षष्टिः ṣaṣṭiḥ [f. nom. sg. ṣaṣṭi] *sixty* तु tu [ind.] *and, but, or, sometimes used as a mere expletive* संजयः saṃjayaḥ [m. nom. sg. saṃjaya] *Saṃjaya, name of the narrator* धृतराष्ट्रः dhṛtarāṣṭraḥ [m. nom. sg. dhṛta-rāṣṭra] *whose empire is firm (name of the king)* श्लोकम् ślokam [m. acc. sg. śloka] *verse* एकम् ekam [m. acc. sg. eka] *one* गीता gītā [f.] *song, sacred song or poem* अया ayā [ind.] *in this manner, thus, in this way, as a result* मान māna [m.] *size, measure in general, dimension, extent* मुच्यते mucyate [3rd sg. pr. pass. √muc] *it is released, loosed, set free*

Krishna spoke 620 verses, Arjuna 57, Sanjaya 67, and Dhritarashtra one verse. In this manner the extent of the Gita is given.

Gītāsāra

GS1 arjuna uvāca |	अर्जुन उवाच ।
yad etan niṣkalaṃ brahma	यदेतन्निष्कलं ब्रह्म
vyomātītaṃ nirañjanam |	व्योमातीतं निरञ्जनम् ।
kaivalyaṃ kevalaṃ śāntaṃ	कैवल्यं केवलं शान्तं
śuddham atyantanirmalam ||	शुद्धमत्यन्तनिर्मलम् ॥

अर्जुनः arjunaḥ [m. nom. sg. arjuna] *Arjuna* उवाच uvāca [3rd sg. perf. act. √vac] *he spoke, said* यद् yad [pron.] *who, which, what, that, whatever;* [n. nom. sg. yad] *as regards, as for* एतद् etad [n. pron.] *this, this here (esp. what is nearest to speaker, this world here below)* निष्कलम् niṣkalam [n. nom. sg. niṣ-kala] *without parts, undivided; nothing (as the opposite of everything: sa-kala)* ब्रह्म brahma [n. nom. sg. brahman] *Brahman, Impersonal Expansion* व्योम vyoma [n. in cpd for vyoman] *sky, heaven, atmosphere* अतीतम् atītaṃ [n. nom. sg. ppp. atī] *past, gone beyond* निरञ्जनम् nirañjanam [n. nom. sg. nir-añjana] *unsmeared, spotless, pure* कैवल्यम् kaivalyam [n. nom. sg. kevala-ya] *perfect isolation; becoming one with the Supreme; beatitude, leading to eternal happiness* केवलम् kevalam [n. nom. sg. kevala] *alone, one, excluding others, whole, all, entire; (ind.) only, merely, solely* शान्तम् śāntam [n. nom. sg. śānta] *gentle, kind, calm, undisturbed; subsided, ceased, stopped, averted* शुद्धम् śuddham [n. nom. sg. ppp. √śudh] *cleansed, pure, bright, white; genuine, true* अत्यन्त atyanta [from aty-anta] *past its proper end or limit, perpetual, perfect* निर्मलम् nirmalam [n. nom. sg. nir-mala] *spotless, shining, bright; sinless, virtuous*

Arjuna spoke:
As for this world here below nothing is Brahman, gone beyond the spotless heaven, an entire undisturbed perfect isolation (Kavailya), genuine, perpetual, virtuous,

GS2 apratarkyam avijñeyaṃ	अप्रतर्क्यमविज्ञेयं
vināśotpattivarjitam |	विनाशोत्पत्तिवर्जितम् ।
jñānayogavinirmuktaṃ	ज्ञानयोगविनिर्मुक्तं
tajjñānaṃ brūhi keśava ||	तज्ज्ञानं ब्रूहि केशव ॥

अप्रतर्क्यम् apratarkyam [n. nom. sg. a-pratarkya] *not to be discussed; incomprehensible by reason, undefinable, unimaginable* अविज्ञेयम् avijñeyam [n. nom. sg. a-vi-jñeya] *not to be perceived or known or understood; unintelligible* विनाश vināśa [m. from vi-√naś] *destruction, annihilation, utter loss* उत्पत्ति utpatti [f. from ud-patti] *arising, birth, origin; becoming visible, coming into existence* वर्जितम् varjitam [n. nom. sg. caus. ppp. √vṛj] *(ifc.) without, deprived of* ज्ञान jñāna [n. from √jñā] *knowing, knowledge* योग yoga *employment, application, performance, striving for Oneness* विनिर्मुक्तम् vinirmuktam [n. nom. sg. vi-nirmukta] *liberated, free from* तज्ज्ञानम् tajjñānam [n. acc. sg. tad-jñāna] *the knowledge of* THAT ब्रूहि brāhi [2nd sg. imperv. act. √brū] *you speak!, you speak about!* केशव keśava [m. voc. sg. keśava] *having long or much or handsom hair, an epithet of Krishna, O Krishna*

unimaginable, unintelligible, annihilation without coming into existence. O Krishna, liberated by Striving for Oneness by knowledge, speak about the knowledge of THAT*!*

GS3 śrībhagavān uvāca |	श्रीभगवानुवाच ।
sarvatojyotir ākāśaṃ	सर्वतोज्योतिराकाशं
sarvabhūtaguṇānvitam |	सर्वभूतगुणान्वितम् ।
sarvataḥparamātmānam	सर्वतःपरमात्मानम्
akṣayaṃ paramaṃ padam ||	अक्षयं परमं पदम् ॥

श्रीभगवान् śrībhagavān [m. nom. sg. bhagavat] *the holy or revered one; the blessed Lord, an epithet of Krishna* उवाच uvāca [3rd sg. perf. act. √vac] *he spoke, said* सर्वतो sarvato [in cpd for sarvatas] *everywhere* ज्योतिः jyotis [n. nom. sg. √jyut] *light, brightness* आकाशम् ākāśam [n. nom. sg. ākāśa] *a free or open space, sky or atmosphere* सर्व sarva [n.] *whole, entire, all, everything* भूत bhūta [n. ppp. √bhū] *that which is or exist, any living being* गुण guṇa [m.] *quality, Basic Attribute* अन्वितम् anvitam [n. nom. sg. anu-ita] *gone along with, linked to, endowed with* सर्वतः sarvataḥ [ind.] *from all sides, entirely* परम parama [superlative of para] *most distant, most excellent, extreme, highest* आत्मानम् ātmānam [m. acc. sg. ātman] *the self, oneself; (ifc.) highest principle of life* अक्षयम् akṣayam [1st sg. imperf. act. √kṣi] *I abided, resided (used esp. of an undisturbed or secret residence)* परमम् paramam [n. acc. sg. parama] *superior, highest, best, most excellent; (ind.) yes, very well* पदम् padam [n. acc. sg. pada] *path, abode, site, home*

Krishna spoke:
Light in the sky everywhere, all beings endowed with the Basic Attributes everywhere, the highest self everywhere, I resided in a superior abode.

GS4 anādinidhanaṃ	अनादिनिधनं
devaṃ mahājyotir atidhruvam |	देवं महाज्योतिरतिध्रुवम् ।
atyantaparamaṃ sthānaṃ	अत्यन्तपरमं स्थानं
śabdādiguṇavarjitam ||	शब्दादिगुणवर्जितम् ॥

अनादि anādi [from an-ādi] *without beginning* निधनम् nidhanam [n. nom. sg. nidhana] *end, loss, any finale* अनादिनिधनम् anādinidhanam [n. nom. sg. an-ādi-nidhana] *having neighter beginning nor end, eternal* देवम् devam [n. nom. sg. deva] *deity, god; heavenly, divine* महा mahā [ibc. for mahat] *great, huge, large, big* ज्योतिस् jyotis [n. from √jyut] *light, brightness* अति ati [ind.] *prefix expressing beyond, excessive* ध्रुवम् dhruvam [n. nom. sg. dhruva] *permanent, firmly fixed, constant, lasting, eternal; an introductory verse, the enduring sound, a repeated prelude* अत्यन्त atyanta [from ati-anta] *past its proper end or limit, endless* परमम् paramam [n. nom. sg. para] *superior* स्थानम् sthānam [n. nom. sg. sthāna] *any place, being fixed or stationary* शब्द śabda [m.] *title; sound, voice, tone* आदि ādi [m.] *(in the middle of cpd) beginning with, and so on* गुण guṇa [m.] *quality, Basic Attribute (Guna); Basic Attribute of the 5 elements (each of which has his own peculiar attributes or attributes as well as organ of sense; thus 1. ether has śabda or sound for its Guna and the ear for its organ; 2. the air has tangibility and sound for its Gunas and the skin for its organ; 3. fire or light has shape or colour, tangibility, and sound for its Gunas, and the eye for its organ; 4. water has flavour, shape, tangibility, and sound for its Gunas, and the tongue for its organ; earth has the preceding Gunas, with the addition of its own peculiar Guna of smell, and the nose for its organ)* वर्जितम् varjitam [n. nom. sg. caus. ppp. √vṛj] *(ifc.) without, deprived of*

The eternal divine great light is beyond the enduring sound, beyond the superior abode, beginning with a sound without Basic Attributes.

GS5 yat tat parataraṃ jyotir	यत्तत्परतरं ज्योतिर्
dhruvāt parataraṃ sthitam |	ध्रुवात्परतरं स्थितम् ।
ācaturyugam adyāpi	आचतुर्युगमद्यापि
kathitaṃ na hi kasyacit ||	कथितं न हि कस्यचित् ॥

यत् yat [pr. act. partc. √i] *going; approaching; arriving at, coming to* तत् tat [n. acc. sg. pron. tad] THAT पर para [adj.] *highest, supreme* परतरम् parataram [n. nom. superlative and comparative of para] *higher or more supreme than* ज्योतिस् jyotis [n. from √jyut] *light, brightness; light as the type of freedom or bliss or victory* पर ज्योतिस् para jyotis *the highest light or truth* ध्रुवात् dhruvāt [n. abl. sg. dhruva] *from or through remaining fixed in one place or constant or firm; through the enduring sound* परतरम् parataram [n. nom. sg. para-tara] *more supreme than* स्थितम् sthitam [n. nom. sg. ppp. √sthā] *to stand firmly, abiding in; being or remaining or keeping in any state or condition* आचतुर्युगम् [n. nom. sg. ā-catur-yuga] *from an era within the four-age cycle: Satya, Tretā, Dvāpara, Kali* अद्यापि adyāpi [ind. a-dya-api] *even now, just now; to this day, henceforth* कथितम् kathitam [n. nom. sg. kathita] *told, said, a discourse* न na [ind.] *not* हि hi [ind.] *for, because, indeed* कस्यचिद् kasyacid [m. sg. gen. kaścid] *of any one*

Coming to THAT, *the ultimate light, is through the ultimate enduring sound state. From an era within the four-age cycle up to this day, it has not been told to anyone.*

GS6 ātmadehe mayā sṛṣṭā prakṛtiḥ kṣetram eva ca | sakalaṃ tu bhavet kṣetraṃ niṣkalaṃ paramaṃ padam ||	आत्मदेहे मया सृष्टा प्रकृतिः क्षेत्रमेव च। सकलं तु भवेत्क्षेत्रं निष्कलं परमं पदम्॥

आत्म ātma [m. in cpd for ātman] *soul, life, self* देहे dehe [m. sg. loc. deha] *in the body, in the embodied one* मया mayā [m. inst. sg. asmad] *by me* सृष्टा sṛṣṭā [f. nom. sg. ppp. √sṛj] *created, produced, brought forth* प्रकृतिः prakṛtiḥ [f. nom. sg. pra-kṛti] *Primordial Substance, nature* क्षेत्रम् kṣetram [n. acc. sg. from √kṣi] *field; sphere of action* एव eva [ind.] *just, as well as, even* च ca [ind.] *and* सकलम् sakalam [n. nom. sg. sa-kala] *all, whole; everything, the whole* तु tu [ind.] *but, and; often an expletive* भवेत् bhavet [3rd sg. pr. opt. act. √bhū] *should, could or would be or become* क्षेत्रम् kṣetram [n. acc. sg. from √kṣi] *field; sphere of action* निष्कलम् niṣkalam [n. nom. sg. niṣ-kala] *without parts, undivided; nothing (opposite of everything: sa-kala)* परमम् paramam [n. nom. sg. para] *superior, ultimate* पदम् padam [n. nom. sg. pada] *path, abode, site, home*

The embodied self is created by Me as well as the Primordial Substance and the field. Everything should become the field; nothing is the superior abode.

GS7 arjuna tvatprasādena śṛṇvantu munisattamaaḥ | adya muktā mahābāho tvatprasādād dhanaṃjaya ||	अर्जुन त्वत्प्रसादेन शृण्वन्तु मुनिसत्तमाः । अद्य मुक्ता महाबाहो त्वत्प्रसादाद्धनंजय॥

अर्जुन arjuna [m. voc. sg. arjuna] *O Arjuna* त्वत् tvat [m. abl. sg. pron. yuṣmad] *from you* प्रसादेन prāsādena [m. inst. sg. prasāda] *by or with clearness, brightness, purity* शृण्वन्तु śṛṇvantu [3rd pl. imperv. act. √śru] *they hear, listen* मुनि muni [m.] *a saint, sage, seer* सत्तमाः sattamāḥ [m. nom. pl. sat-tama] *very good, the best, first* अद्य adya [ind.] *today, now* मुक्ताः muktāḥ [3rd pl. ppp. √muc] *they liberated, emancipated* महाबाहो mahābāho [m. voc. sg. mahābāhu] *O mighty armed one, epithet of Arjuna* त्वत् tvat [m. abl. sg. yuṣmad] *from you* प्रसादात् prasādāt [m. abl. sg. prasāda] *from clearness, brightness, purity* धनम्जय dhanaṃjaya [m. voc. sg. dhana-ṃ-jaya] *O winner of wealth, epithet of Arjuna*

O Arjuna, they hear with clarity from you, the best of sages! Now they are liberated, O Mighty Armed One, due to clarity from you, O Winner of Wealth.

GS8 pramāṇaṃ vedatattvānāṃ sāṃkhyādīny abhiyoginām | teṣāṃ na vidyate niṣṭhā sarvaiḥ pāṣaṇḍibhiḥ saha ||	प्रमाणं वेदतत्त्वानां सांख्यादीन्यभियोगिनाम् । तेषां न विद्यते निष्ठा सर्वैः पाषण्डिभिः सह ॥

प्रमाणम् pramāṇam [n. nom. sg. pra-māna] *measure; authority; right perception; means of acquiring certain knowledge* वेद veda [m. from √vid] *knowledge, true or sacred knowledge* तत्त्वानाम् tattvānām [n. gen. pl. tattva] *of truth, true states, realities* सांख्य sāṃkhya [m.] *Samkhya philosophy* आदीनि ādīni [n. pl. nom. ādi] *beginnings* अभियोगिनाम् abhiyoginām [n. gen. pl. abhiyogin] *of intent upon, absorbed in attacking* तेषाम् teṣām [n. gen. pl. pron. tad] *of them, their; of these, those* न na [ind.] *not* विद्यते vidyate [3rd sg. pr. indic. pass. √vid] *it is found, there is* निष्ठा niṣṭhā [f.] *state, condition, position; firmness, steadiness, attachment, devotion, application; completion, perfection; conclusion, end* सर्वैः sarvaiḥ [n. inst. pl. sarva] *with or by all* पाषण्डिभिः pāṣaṇḍibhiḥ [m. inst. pl. pāṣaṇḍin] *with or by heretics* सह saha [ind.] *together, with; conjointly*

There is no application of the right perception of sacred knowledge, of truth, of focus on the beginnings of the Samkhya philosophy by all the heretics together.

GS9 kathitaṃ ca mayā jñānaṃ devānām api durlabham | viśvarūpamayaṃ divyaṃ bhairavagranthibindunā ||	कथितं च मया ज्ञानं देवानामपि दुर्लभम्। विश्वरूपमयं दिव्यं भैरवग्रन्थिबिन्दुना॥

कथितम् kathitam [m. acc. sg. kathita] *told, said, a discourse* च ca [ind.] *and; often a more expletive* मया mayā [m. inst. sg. asmad] *by me* ज्ञानम् jñānam [n. nom. sg. jñāna] *knowing, knowledge* देवानाम् devānām [m. gen. pl. deva] *of the gods* अपि api [adv.] *and, moreover, also, besides* दुर्लभम् durlabham [n. nom. sg. durlabham] *difficult to be obtained or found, rare* विश्व viśva [adj.] *all, universal; all-pervading or all-containing* रूप rūpa [n.] *form, shape, figure* मयम् mayam [m. acc. sg. maya] *suffix denoting formed from, made of, developed* दिव्यम् divyam [n. nom. sg. div-ya] *divine, heavenly* भैरव bhairava [m.] *formidable, terrific; relating to Bhairava (a form of Shiva)* ग्रन्थि granthi [m.] *a knot, a tie, a bunch of any kind* बिन्दुना bindunā [n. inst. sg. bindu] *by or with a detached particle; by or with a drop, a point, dot (is considered as the point at which creation begins)*

Besides, the knowledge of the gods told by Me is difficult to find. The divine universal form is developed by the dot knot related to Bhairava.

GS10 suṣumṇā dakṣiṇe mārge
darśitā viśvarūpiṇā |
aprakāśam idaṃ praśnaṃ
yan mayā kathitaṃ tava ||

सुषुम्णा दक्षिणे मार्गे
दर्शिता विश्वरूपिणा।
अप्रकाशमिदं प्रश्नं
यन्मया कथितं तव॥

सुषुम्णा suṣumṇā [f. nom. sg. su-ṣumṇa] *very gracious or kind, a particular artery or vein of the body supposed to be one of the passages for the breath or spirit; the central subtle channel* दक्षिणे dakṣiṇe [n. loc. sg. dakṣiṇa] *in or on the path, way through, able, skillful, right (not left), south, southern (as being on the right side of a person looking eastward), situated to the south, turned or directed southward; straightforward; straightforward, sincere; (ind.) on the right* मार्गे mārge [n. loc. sg. mārga] *in or on any track, road, path, way to* दर्शिता darśitā [f. nom. sg. darśita] *shown, displayed; explained; seen, understood; visible, apparent* विश्व viśva [adj.] *all, universal; all-pervading or all-containing* रूपिणा rūpiṇā [n. inst. sg. rūpin] *with or by having a (beautiful) form, handsome, well-shaped; (ifc.) having the form or nature or character of, characterised by, appearing as* अप्रकाशम् aprakāśam [n. acc. sg. a-prakāśa] *not shining, dark; not visible, hidden, secret* इदम् idam [ind.] *now, just, even; in this manner; this, this here* प्रश्नम् praśnam [m. acc. sg. praśna] *a question, demand, inquiry, a subject of inquiry* यद् yad [pron.] *who, which, what, that*; [n. nom. sg. yad] *as for, as regards* मया mayā [m. inst. sg. asmad] *by or with me* कथितम् kathitam [n. acc. sg. kathita] *told, said, a discourse, conversation* तव tava [m. gen. sg. yuṣmad] *of you, your*

The central subtle channel on the southern path is understood by its universal nature. As for this secret question, your discourse is with Me.

GS11 nāgnir vāyur na cākāśaṃ
na kṣitir nāpi vā jalam |
na manobuddhyahaṃkāraṃ
gūḍhārthaṃ kathitaṃ tava ||

नाग्निर्वायुर्न चाकाशं
न क्षितिर्नापि वा जलम् ।
न मनोबुद्ध्यहंकारं
गूढार्थं कथितं तव

न na [ind.] *not* अग्निः agniḥ [m. nom. sg. agni] *fire, sacrificial fire; the god of fire* वायुः vāyuḥ [m. nom. sg. vāyu] *wind, air; the god of the wind* न na [ind.] *not* च ca [ind.] *and* आकाशम् ākāśam [n. nom. sg. ākāśa] *light, clearness; free open space, ether* न na [ind.] *not* क्षितिर् kṣitir [m. nom. sg. kṣiti] *abode, dwelling, residence, house; the earth, the soil of the earth* न na [ind.] *not* अपि api [adv.] *and, moreover, also, besides, even* वा vā [ind.] *or* जलम् jalam [n. acc. sg. jala] *water, any fluid; cold, stupid, ideotic* न na [ind.] *not* मनस् manas [n.] *mind, intellect, understanding, consciousness; judging or determining (Samkhya)* बुद्धि buddhi [f.] *intelligence, the power of forming and retaining conceptions and general notions; ascertainment (Samkhya)* अहंकारम् ahaṃkāram [m. acc. sg. ahaṃkāra] *I-making, conception of one's individuality; egotism; self-consciousness (Samkhya)* गूढ gūḍha [adj.] *covered, hidden, concealed, secret* अर्थम् artham [n. acc. sg. artha] *cause, motive, reason; having to do with; aim, purpose; (ind.) on account of, in behalf of* कथितम् kathitam [n. acc. sg. kathita] *told, said, a discourse, conversation* तव tava [m. gen. sg. yuṣmad] *of you, your*

Not fire, air and ether, not earth or even water, not mind, intelligence or self-consciousness is the secret reason of your discourse.

GS12 anityo nityatāṃ yāti
yadā bhāvaṃ na paśyati |
śūnyaṃ nirañjanākāraṃ
nirvāṇaṃ dhruvam avyayam ||

अनित्यो नित्यतां याति
यदा भावं न पश्यति ।
शून्यं निरञ्जनाकारं
निर्वाणं ध्रुवमव्ययम् ॥

अनित्यः anityaḥ [m. nom. sg. anitya] *not everlasting, incidental, transient* नित्यताम् nityatām [f. acc. sg. nityatā] *perpetuity, continuance* याति yāti [3rd sg. pr. indic. act. √yā] *he goes, goes to any state or condition, becomes, is (eps. with the acc. of an abstract noun); reaches, enters, approaches, arrives at, comes to; discovers, undertakes, undergoes (acc.)* यदा yadā [ind.] *when, at that time* भावम् bhāvam [m. acc. sg. bhāva] *that which is or exist, being; becoming, existing* न na [ind.] *not* पश्यति paśyati [3rd sg. pr. indic. act. √paś] *he sees, perceives* शून्यम् śūnyam [n. nom. sg. śūnya] *empty, void; non-existent; vacuum, blank; space, heaven, ether (ether has śabda or sound for its Guna and the ear for its organ), the sky; vacant, void of, free from* निरञ्जन nirañjana [m.n.] *unpainted, spotless, pure, simple* अकारम् akāram [m. acc. sg. a-kāra] *the letter or sound Aa, sounding Aa (the first vowel)* निर्वाणम् nirvāṇam [n. acc. sg. nirvāṇa] *blowing out, extinction, bliss* ध्रुवम् dhruvam [n. nom. sg. dhruva] *permanent, firmly fixed, constant, lasting, eternal; an introductory verse, the enduring sound, a repeated prelude* अव्ययम् avyayam [n. nom. sg. avyaya] *imperishable, changeless*

One goes to incidental continuance when one does not see that which exists. The ether is sounding a pure Aa, the enduring sound of imperishable bliss.

GS13 puruṣaṃ nirguṇaṃ sākṣāt
sarvataś caiva tiṣṭhati |
sarvaṃ tat syāt paraṃ brahma
buddhiś cāsya na budhyati ||

पुरुषं निर्गुणं साक्षात्
सर्वतश्चैव तिष्ठति ।
सर्वं तत्स्यात्परं ब्रह्म
बुद्धिश्चास्य न बुध्यति ॥

पुरुषम् puruṣam [n. nom. sg. puruṣa] *man, male, human being, mankind; the Supreme Being or Soul of the Universe* निर्गुणम् nirguṇam [n. nom. sg. nir-guṇa] *without Basic Attributes (Gunas); missing virtues; worthless, vicious, bad* साक्षात् sākṣāt [n. abl. sg. sākṣa] *from having eyes; (ind.) before the eyes, in sight of; evidently, with one's own eyes* सर्वतः sarvataḥ [ind.] *from all sides, entirely* च ca [ind.] *and, also, just, as well as; even, indeed, both, likewise* एव eva [ind.] *just, as well as, even* तिष्ठति tiṣṭhati [3rd sg. pr. indic. act. √sthā] *it remains, stands, stays; it is engaged in; it continues in any condition or action* सर्वम् sarvam [n. nom. sg. pron. sarva] *whole, entire, all* तत् tat [n. nom. sg. pron. tad] *that* स्यात् syāt [ind.] *it may be, perhaps* परम् param [n. nom. sg. para] *highest, supreme* ब्रह्म brahma [n. nom. sg. brahman] *Brahman, Impersonal Expansion* बुद्धिः buddhiḥ [f. nom. sg. buddhi] *intelligence, the power of forming and retaining conceptions and general notions* च [ind.] *and* अस्य asya [n. gen. sg. idam] *of this, of this here* न na [ind.] *not* बुध्यति budhyati [3rd sg. pr. indic. act. √budh] *he is awake, aware; he perveives, he notices, understands*

Evidently without Basic Attributes, mankind continues entirely as before. The supreme intelligence of Brahman is perhaps all that is, and of this [mankind] is not aware.

GS14 pratibhāvaprayatnena
harim trailokyabāndhavam |
daśamam cāṅgulam vyāpya
cāśābāhyam vyavasthitam ||

प्रतिभावप्रयत्नेन
हरिं त्रैलोक्यबान्धवम् ।
दशमं चाङ्गुलं व्याप्य
चाशाबाह्यं व्यवस्थितम् ॥

प्रति prati *a prefix expressing towards, near to, against, in opposion to* प्रति-भाव pratibhāva [m.] *counterpart* प्रयत्नेन prayatnena [m. inst. sg. prayatna] *by or with persevering effort, continued exertion or endeavour* हरिम् harim [m. acc. sg. hari] *horse, steed, a lion; epithet of Vishnu-Krishna, Shiva, etc.* त्रैलोक्य trailokya [n.] *the three worlds* बान्धवम् bāndhavam [m. acc. sg. bāndava] *a kinsman, relation, friend* दशमम् daśamam [ind.] *for the tenth time* च ca [ind.] *and, both, as well as* अङ्गुलम् aṅgulam [m. acc. sg. aṅgula] *a finger, the thumb, the measure of a finger's breadth* व्याप्य vyāpya [ind., caus. abs. vi-√āp] *after having reached or spread through, pervaded, permeated, covered, filled* [gerund vyāp] *reaching or spreading through, pervading, covering, filling* च ca [ind.] *and; a double ca may be used somewhat redundantly* आशा āśā *space, region, quarter of heaven* अबाह्यम् abāhyam [n. nom. sg. a-bāhya] *not external, internal; without an exterior* व्यवस्थितम् vyavasthitam [n. nom. sg. vi-ava-sthita] *placed in order; placed, put, situated; proving, appearing as; fixed, settled; one who has waited or stayed; standing near*

The relation of the three worlds and Krishna is without persevering effort, having been reached through the measure of a finger's breadth for the tenth time and staying in internal space.

GS15 jīvo yatra pralīyeta sā kalā ṣoḍaśī smṛtā | tayā sarvam idaṃ vyāptaṃ trailokyaṃ sacarācaram ||	जीवो यत्र प्रलीयेत सा कला षोडशी स्मृता । तया सर्वमिदं व्याप्तं त्रैलोक्यं सचराचरम् ॥

जीवः jīvaḥ [m. nom. sg. jīva] *any living being, life, the principle of life, the living or personal soul* यत्र yatra [ind.] *in or to which place, where, in which case, if, when* प्रलीय pralīya [ind. abs. pra-√lī] *after having becoming dissolved, disappeared, perished, died* इत ita [ppp. √i] *gone; returned; obtained* सा sā [f. nom. sg. pron. tad] *this* कला kalā [f. nom. sg. kalā] *a small part of anything, any single part or portion of a whole, esp. a sixteenth part; an atom* कलाः kalāḥ [f. nom. pl. kala] *low, soft (as a tone, emitting soft tones, melodious (as a voice or throat)* षोडशी ṣoḍaśī [f. nom. sg. ṣoḍaśin] *consisting of sixteen; having sixteen parts* कला षोडशी kalā ṣoḍaśī *the whole (a sixteenth part sixteen times)* स्मृता smṛtā [f. nom. sg. smṛta] *handed down (by memory), taught, prescribed* तया tayā [f. inst. sg. tad] *by that* सर्वम् sarvam [n. nom. sg. pron. sarva] *whole, entire, all* इदम् idam [ind.] *now, just, even; in this manner* व्याप्तम् vyāptam [n. nom. sg. vyāpta] *spread through, pervaded, thoroughly penetrated by* त्रैलोक्यम् trailokyam [n. nom. sg. trai-lokya] *the three worlds* सचराचरम् sacarācaram [n. nom. sg. sa-cara-acara] *the moving and unmoving*

After having disappeared when the living soul returned to this prescribed whole, the moving and unmoving are now pervaded by the three worlds.

GS16 tac cintyaṃ tena vai jñānaṃ	तच्चिन्त्यं तेन वै ज्ञानं
tad atrādyā upāsate |	तदत्राद्या उपासते।
brahmaṇaiva hi vikhyātaṃ	ब्रह्मणैव हि विख्यातं
vedānteṣu prakāśitam ||	वेदान्तेषु प्रकाशितम्॥

तत् tat [n. nom. sg. pron. tad] *that* चिन्त्यम् cintyam [n. nom. sg. cintya] *to be thought about or imagined; to be thought of, to be considered or meditated upon; the necessity of thinking about anything; questionable* तेन tena [n. inst. sg. tad] *by that* वै vai [ind.] *particle of emphasis: "indeed, truly, verily, just"* ज्ञानम् jñānam [n. nom. sg. jñāna] *knowing, knowledge* तत् tat [n. nom. sg. pron. tad] *that* अत्र atra [ind.] *in this respect; in this place, here; at this time; then* आद्याः ādyāḥ [f. acc. pl. ādya] *the beginnings* उपासते upāsate [3rd pl. pr. indic. mid. √upās] *they are devoted to, honour, worship, respect* ब्रह्मणा bramaṇā [n. inst. sg. brahman] *by Impersonal Expansion, by Brahman* एव eva [ind.] *just, as well as, even* हि hi [ind.] *for, because; certainly; a mere expletive* विख्यातम् vikhyātam [n. nom. sg. vikhyāta] *generally known, known as, called, named* वेदान्तेषु vedānteṣu [m. loc. pl. veda-anta] *in the end of the Vedas, in complete knowledge of the Vedas; Vedanta philosophy* प्रकाशितम् prakāśitam [n. acc. sg. prakāśita] *become visible, apparent, evident, manifest; illuminated, enlightened*

To be meditated upon THAT *with* THAT *is knowledge indeed. Then they respect* THAT *beginnings, known by Brahman and illuminated in the complete knowledge of the Vedas.*

GS17	vedeṣu vedam ity āhur vedadhāma paraṃ matam | tatparaṃ viditaṃ yasya sa vipro vedapāragaḥ ||	वेदेषु वेदमित्याहुर् वेदधाम परं मतम्। तत्परं विदितं यस्य स विप्रो वेदपारगः॥

वेदेषु vedeṣu [m. loc. pl. veda] *in the Vedas* वेदम् vedam [m. acc. sg. veda] *knowledge, true or sacred knowledge* इति iti [ind.] *in this manner, thus, marks a quotation* आहुः āhuḥ [3rd pl. perf. indic. act. √ah] *they say, call* वेद veda [m. from √vid] *knowledge, true or sacred knowledge* धाम dhāma [n. acc. sg. dhāman] *abode, house, domain* परम् param [n. nom. sg. para] *highest, supreme* मतम् matam [n. nom. sg. ppp. √man] *thought, considered as, idea, doctrine* तत् tat [n. nom. sg. pron. tad] *that* परम् param [n. nom. sg. para] *highest, supreme* विदितम् viditam [n. nom. sg. vidita] *known, understood; knowledge* यस्य yasya [n. gen. sg. yad] *whose, of who, of what* सः saḥ [m. nom. sg. pron. tad] *he* विप्रः vipraḥ [m. nom. sg. vipra] *singer of hymns, a sage, seer* वेद veda [m. from √vid] *knowledge, true or sacred knowledge* पारगः pāragaḥ [m. nom. sg. pāra-ga] *one who has gone through or accomplished or mastered, knowing thoroughly, profoundly learned*

They say: "The sacred knowledge in the Vedas" is the abode of true knowledge and the supreme thought of whoever has understood the supreme THAT. *He is a sage who has mastered true knowledge.*

GS18 āhutiḥ sā parā jñeyā
sā ca saṃdhyā pratiṣṭhitā |
gāyatrī sā parā jñeyā
ajapā nāma viśrutā ||

आहुतिः सा परा ज्ञेया
सा च संध्या प्रतिष्ठिता ।
गायत्री सा परा ज्ञेया
अजपा नाम विश्रुता॥

आहुतिः āhutiḥ [f. nom. sg. āhuti] *delighting in sacrifices; offering oblations with fire to the deities; any solemn rite accompanied with oblations; calling, invoking* सा sā [f. nom. sg. tad] *she, it, this* परा parā [f. nom. sg. para] *farther than, beyond; highest, supreme, chief* ज्ञेया jñeyā [f. nom. sg. fpp. √jñā] *to be known, to be learnt or understood or perceived* सा sā [f. nom. sg. tad] *she, it, this* च ca [ind.] *and, as well as* संध्या saṃdhyā [f. nom. sg. saṃdhyā] *holding together, union, junction; religious acts performed by brahmins in morning, noon and evening esp. a Gāyatrī prayer* प्रतिष्ठिता pratiṣṭhitā [f. nom. sg. pratiṣṭhitā] *established, proved* गायत्री gāyatrī [f. nom. sg. gāyatrī] *any hymn composed in the ancient meter of 24 syllables, often a triplet of eight syllables each* सा sā [f. nom. sg. tad] *she, it, this* परा parā [f. nom. sg. para] *farther than, beyond; highest, supreme, chief* ज्ञेया jñeyā [f. nom. sg. fpp. √jñā] *to be known, to be learnt or understood or perceived* अजपा ajapā [f. nom. sg. ajapā] *the mantra or formula called haṃsa (goose, swan, the vehicle of Brahman), which consists only of a number of inhalations and exhalations* नाम nāma [ind.] *by name, named, called; indeed, certainly* विश्रुता viśrutā [f. nom. sg. vi-śruta] *heard of far and wide, noted, renowned, celebrated, famous, well known; pleased, happy*

This offering is the highest to be known, and is an established religious act. This is the supreme, most famous Gayatri hymn named Hamsa, the vehicle of Brahman.

GS19 tapasy atha tathā vede
munibhiḥ samupāsyate |
tāṃ kalāṃ yo 'bhijānāti
sa kalājño 'bhidhīyate ||

तपस्य् अथ तथा वेदे
मुनिभिः समुपास्यते ।
तां कलां यो ऽभिजानाति
स कलाज्ञो ऽभिधीयते ॥

तपसि tapasi [n. loc.abs. sg. tapas] *in suffering; in religious austerity* अथ atha [ind.] *now, then; certainly; what?* तथा tathā [ind.] *so also, likewise; so, thus* वेदे vede [m. loc.abs. sg. veda] *in the Veda; in the knowledge of ritual* मुनिभिः munibhiḥ [m. inst. pl. muni] *by the seers, sages, devotees* समुपास्यते samupāsyate [3rd sg. pr. indic. pass. sam-upa-√ās] *it is honored or served together; one worships; one sits near together or near each other; one engages in or devotes one's self to anything together, practises in common or singly* ताम् tām [f. acc. sg. tad] *her, this* कलाम् kalām [f. acc. sg. kalā] *a small part of anything, any single part or portion of a whole, esp. a sixteenth part; an atom* यः yaḥ [m. nom. sg. yad] *who, what, which* अभिजानाति abhijānāti [3rd sg. pr. indic. act. abhi-√jñā] *he/she knows understands, is aware of, apprehends* सः saḥ [m. nom. sg. pron. tad] *that, he* कला kalā [f.] *a small part of anything; an atom* ज्ञः jñaḥ [m. nom. sg. jña] *knowing, familiar with; a wise and learned man; the thinking soul* अज्ञः ajñaḥ [m. nom. sg. a-jña] *not knowing, not familiar with; ignorant, inexperienced, unwise, stupid* अभिधीयते abhidhīyate [3rd sg. pr. indic. pass. abhi-√dhā] *to be named or called*

Certainly, religious austerity is thus when the Veda is honored by the sages. Whoever understands this small part, he is called one who is learned of a small part.

GS20 yāṃ jñātvā mucyate jantur garbhajanmajarādibhiḥ | parijñānena mucyante narāḥ pātakakilbiṣaiḥ ||	यां ज्ञात्वा मुच्यते जन्तुर् गर्भजन्मजरादिभिः । परिज्ञानेन मुच्यन्ते नराः पातककिल्बिषैः ॥

याम् yām [f. acc. sg. pron. yad] *who, which* ज्ञात्वा jñātvā [abs. √jñā] *after having known, knowing* मुच्यते mucyate [3rd sg. pr. indic. pass. √muc] *he is loosed, he is set free, is released, becomes free* जन्तुः jantuḥ [m. nom. sg. jantu] *a creature, living being, person, man; also used collectively* गर्भ garbha [m.] *the womb, belly, the inside, embryo, child, impregnation* जन्म janma [in cpd for janman] *birth, production, origin, life; birthplace, home* जरा jarā [f.] *old age, the act of becoming old* आदिभिः ādibhiḥ [f. inst. pl. ādi] *(ifc.) by the beginnings with, and so on* परिज्ञानेन parijñānena [n. inst. sg. pari-jñāna] *by perception, with thorough knowledge, experience* मुच्यन्ते mucyante [3rd pl. pr. indic. pass. √muc] *they are loosed, they are set free or released, they become free* नराः narāḥ [m. nom. pl. nara] *men, people* पातक pātaka [n.] *causing to fall, that which causes to fall or sink; sin* किल्बिषैः kilbiṣaiḥ [n. inst. pl. kilbiṣa] *by faults, offences, sin, guilt*

Those knowing who is released by a life from childhood to old age are men with thorough knowledge. Many are released by knowing the faults that cause one to fall.

GS21 iḍā bhagavatī gaṅgā piṅgalā yamunā nadī | tayor madhye tṛtīyā tu tat prayāgam anusmaret ||	इडा भगवती गङ्गा पिङ्गला यमुना नदी। तयोर्मध्ये तृतीया तु तत्प्रयागमनुस्मरेत्॥

इडा iḍā [f. nom. sg. iḍā] *vital spirit, left channel for vital spirit* भगवती bhagavatī [f. nom. sg. bhagavat] *divine or adorable one, name of Laksmi, (m.) Krishna* गङ्गा gaṅgā [f. nom. sg. gaṅgā] *"swift-goer", the river Ganges* पिङ्गला piṅgalā [f. nom. sg. piṅgala] *right channel for vital spirit, for breath and air* यमुना yamunā [f. nom. sg. yamunā (from 'yama')] *"twin", the river Yamuna* नदी nadī [f. nom. sg. nadī] *flowing water, a river, a stream* तयोः tayoḥ [f. gen.loc. du. tad] *in/of that two* मध्ये madhye [f. nom. du. madhya] *the middle, midst, between; space between* तृतीया tṛtīyā [f. nom. sg. tṛtīyā] *the third* तु tu [ind.] *but, and; often an expletive* तत् tat [n. acc. sg. pron. tad] *that* प्रयागम् prayāgam [m. acc. sg. prayāga] *place of sacrifice* अनुस्मरेत् anusmaret [3rd sg. pr. opt. act. anu-√smṛ] *he should remember; may he remember*

The left channel for the vital spirit is like the divine river Ganges, the right channel for the vital spirit is like the river Yamuna, but between these two is the third, and one should remember that place of sacrifice.

GS22 iḍā vai vaiṣṇavī nāḍī brahmanāḍī tu piṅgalā | suṣumṇā caiśvarī nāḍī tridhā prāṇavahā smṛtā | brahmā viṣṇur mahādevo recakaḥ pūrakumbhakaḥ ||	इडा वै वैष्णवी नाडी ब्रह्मनाडी तु पिङ्गला । सुषुम्णा चैश्वरी नाडी त्रिधा प्राणवहा स्मृता । ब्रह्मा विष्णुर्महादेवो रेचकः पूरकुम्भकः ॥

इडा iḍā [f. nom. sg. iḍā] *vital spirit, left channel for vital spirit* वै vai [ind.] *particle of emphasis: "indeed, truly, verily, just"* वैष्णवी vaiṣṇavī [f. nom. sg. vaiṣṇava] *related or belonging to Vishnu; worshipping Vishnu* नाडी nāḍī [f. nom. sg. nāḍī] *any pipe or tube; subtle channel through which the life force circulates* ब्रह्म brahma [n. nom. sg. brahman] *Brahman, Impersonal Expansion* नाडी nāḍī [f. nom. sg. nāḍī] *subtle channel* तु tu [ind.] *but, and; often an expletive* पिङ्गला piṅgalā [f. nom. sg. piṅgala] *right channel for vital spirit, for breath and air* सुषुम्णा suṣumṇā [f. nom. sg. suṣumṇa] *very gratious or kind; central or middle channel for vital spirit* च ca [ind.] *and, both, likewise* इश्वरी īśvarī [f. nom. sg. īśvara] *capable of, able to do; master, mistress, queen; Supreme Being; name of female energies of the deities* नाडी nāḍī [f. nom. sg. nāḍī] *subtle channel* त्रिधा tridhā [ind.] *in three ways, parts, places; triply* प्राण prāṇa [m.] *the breath of life, spirit, respiration; vital energy, a vital organ* वहा vahā [f. nom. sg. vaha] *(ifc.) carrying, bearing, conveying, bringing, causing, producing* स्मृता smṛtā [f. nom. sg. smṛta] *handed down (by memory), taught, prescribed* ब्रह्मा brahmā [f. nom. sg. brahman] *Brahman, Impersonal Expansion* विष्णुः viṣṇuḥ [f.m. nom. sg. viṣṇu] *"All-pervader or Worker," Vishnu (regarded as "the preserver")* महादेवः mahādeva [m. nom. sg. mahādeva] *the great deity, name of Shiva* रेचकः recakaḥ [m. nom. sg. recaka] *expelling the breath out of one of the nostrils* पूर pūra [m.] *the act of filling, fullfilling; the swelling or rising of a river or of the sea, stream; a kind of breath exercise (closing the right nostril with the forefinger and inhale through the left nostril then reverse left and right, and repeat)* कुम्भकः kumbhakaḥ [m.n. nom. sg. kumbhaka] *stopping the breath by shutting the mouth and closing the nostrils with the fingers of the right hand*

The left channel for the vital spirit is indeed related to Vishnu's subtle channel, the right channel to Brahman's subtle channel, and the middle channel is the subtle channel for the female energies of the deities. The three, carrying the breath of life, call to mind Brahman, Vishnu, and Shiva, and the three breath exercises, recaka, pura, and kumbhaka.

GS23 sakrāntiviṣuvac caiva	सक्रान्तिविषुवच्चैव
yo 'bhijānāti vigraham |	यो ऽभिजानाति विग्रहम् ।
nityayuktaḥ sa yogīśo	नित्ययुक्तः स योगीशो
brahmavidyāṃ prapadyate ||	ब्रह्मविद्यां प्रपद्यते ॥

स sa [ind. prefix] *together, with; together or along with; "having the same"* क्रान्ति krānti [f. nom. sg. krānta] *going,* विषुवत् viṣuvat [n. nom. sg. viṣuvat] *having or sharing both sides equally, being in the middle, central; top, summit, vertex* च ca [ind.] *and, both, likewise* एव eva [ind.] *just, as well as, even* यः yaḥ [m. nom. sg. yad] *who, what, which* अभिजानाति abhijānāti [3rd sg. pr. indic. act. abhi-√jñā] *he knows, understands, is aware of, apprehends* विग्रहम् vigraham [m. acc. sg. vigraha] *discord, quarrel, contest, war; separate; keeping apart or asunder, isolation, division* नित्ययुक्तः nityayuktaḥ [m. nom. sg. nitya-yukta] *always busy or fixed upon one subject or intent upon* सः saḥ [m. nom. sg. pron. tad] *he* योगी yogī [m. nom. sg. yogin] *a yogi, a Striver for Oneness* ईशः īśaḥ [m. nom. sg. īśa] *owning, possessing, sharing, one who is completely master of anything; powerful, supreme; a ruler, master, lord; name of Shiva* ब्रह्मविद्याम् brahmavidyām [f. acc. sg. brahma-vidyā] *knowledge of Impersonal Expansion* प्रपद्यते prapadyate [3rd sg. pr. indic. mid. pra-√pad] *he attains, resorts to, takes refuge with, enters*

Whoever is aware of division is going in the middle. He is a powerful Striver for Oneness, always fixed upon one subject and resorts to the knowledge of Brahman.

GS24 iḍā vai gārhapatyas tu piṅgalāhavanīyakaḥ | suṣumṇā dakṣiṇāgnis tu hy etad agnitrayaṃ smṛtam ||	इडा वै गार्हपत्यस्तु पिङ्गलाहवनीयकः । सुषुम्णा दक्षिणाग्निस्तु ह्येतदग्नित्रयं स्मृतम् ॥

इडा iḍā [f. nom. sg. iḍā] *vital spirit, left channel for vital spirit* वै vai [ind.] *particle of emphasis: "indeed, truly, verily, just"* गार्हपत्यः gārhapatyaḥ [m. nom. sg. gārha-patya] *the householder's fire (received from his father from which the sacrificial fires are lighted), usually the western fire of the altar; a household* तु tu [ind.] *but, and; often an expletive* पिङ्गला piṅgalā [f. nom. sg. piṅgala] *right channel for the vital spirit, for breath and air* आहवनीयकः āhavanīyakaḥ [m. nom. sg. āhavanīyaka] *the eastern fire of the altar offered as an oblation and taken from the householder's perpetual fire* सुषुम्णा suṣumṇā [f. nom. sg. suṣumṇa] *very gratious or kind; central or middle channel for vital spirit* दक्षिणाग्निः dakṣiṇāgniḥ [m. nom. sg. dakṣiṇa-āgni] *the southern fire of the altar* तु tu [ind.] *but, and; often an expletive* हि hi [ind.] *for, because; certainly; a mere expletive* एतद् etad [n. pron.] *this, this here, this world here below* अग्नित्रयम् agnitrayam [n. nom. sg. agnitraya] *the three sacred fires* स्मृतम् smṛtam [n. nom. sg. smṛta] *handed down (by memory), taught, thought of, prescribed (eps. enjoined by traditional law, declared or propounded in the law-books)*

Truly, the left channel for the vital spirit and the western fire of the altar, the right channel for the vital spirit and the eastern fire of the altar, the middle channel for the vital spirit and the southern fire of the altar, prescribed the three sacred fires.

GS25	tasya madhye sthitaṃ jyotiḥ	तस्य मध्ये स्थितं ज्योतिः
	somamaṇḍalam eva ca |	सोममण्डलमेव च ।
	somamaṇḍalamadhyasthaṃ	सोममण्डलमध्यस्थं
	tanmadhye sūryamaṇḍalam ||	तन्मध्ये सूर्यमण्डलम् ॥

तस्य tasya [n. gen. sg. pron. tad] *of him, his, for him, of this, its* **मध्ये** madhye [n. loc. sg. madhya] *in the middle, midst, between; space between; within* **स्थितम्** sthitam [n. nom. sg. ppp. √sthā] *standing firmly, abiding in; situated, resting in, keeping in any state or condition* **ज्योतिस्** jyotis [n. from √jyut] *light, brightness* **सोम** soma [m.] *juice, extract, esp., the juice of the Soma plant* **मण्डलम्** maṇḍalam [n. nom. sg. maṇḍala] *anything round, a circle, ring, circumference, wheel; surrounding district or neighbouring state* **एव** eva [ind.] *just, as well as, even, a mere expletive* **च** ca [ind.] *and, both, likewise* **सोममण्डल** somamaṇḍala [n.] *Soma circle* **मध्यस्थम्** madhyastham [n. nom. sg. madhya-stha] *being in the middle, being between; belonging to neither or both parties; impartial, neutral, indifferent; being in a middle condition or kind; being in the air* **तन्मध्ये** tanmadhye [n. loc. sg. tan-madhya] *in the midst thereof* **सूर्यमण्डलम्** sūryamaṇḍalam [n. nom. sg. sūrya-maṇḍala] *the orb or disk of the sun*

He stands firmly within the light and the Soma circle. The Soma circle is in the middle, and in the midst thereof is the disk of the Sun.

GS26 sūryamaṇḍalamadhyastho jvalat tejo hutāśanaḥ | hutāśanasya madhye tu nirdhūmāñgāravarcasam ||	सूर्यमण्डलमध्यस्थो ज्वलत्तेजो हुताशनः । हुताशनस्य मध्ये तु निर्धूमाङ्गारवर्चसम् ॥

सूर्यमण्डल sūryamaṇḍala [from sūrya-maṇḍala] *the orb or disk of the sun* मध्यस्थः madhyasthaḥ [m. nom. sg. madhya-stha] *being in the middle, being between; belonging to neither or both parties; impartial, neutral, indifferent; being in a middle condition or kind* ज्वलत् jvalat [n. nom. sg. jvalat: pr. act. partc. √jval] *blazing fire, flame; burning brightly, shining, glowing* तेजस् tejas [n. nom. sg. teja] *point or top of a flame or ray, glow, glare, splendor, brilliance, light, fire; fiery energy, vital power* हुत huta [mfn.] *offered in fire, poured out (as clarified butter), burnt (as an oblation), sacrificed; sacrificed to, one to whom an oblation is offered; (n.) an oblation, offering, sacrifice* अशनः aśanaḥ [m. nom. sg. aśana] *(ifc.) having roots and fruit for food* हुताशनस्य hutāśanasya [m. gen. sg. hutāśana] *of food offered in fire; food offered has* मध्ये madhye [ind.] *in the middle, midst, within, between; among, in the presence of* तु tu [ind.] *but, and, then, now; often an expletive* निर्धूम nirdhūma [mfn.] *free of smoke, smokeless* अङ्गार añgāra [m.] *charcoal, either heated or not heated* वर्चसम् varcasam [n. nom. sg. varcasa] *(ifc.) light, lustre, colour*

The disk of the sun is between the glow of the flames and the offering of food. In the middle of the food offered is light from smokeless charcoal.

GS27 tatrāsthito mahātmāsau yogibhis tu pragīyate | sugītaṃ caiva kartavyaṃ mana ekāgracetasā ||	तत्रास्थितो महात्मासौ योगिभिस्तु प्रगीयते । सुगीतं चैव कर्तव्यं मन एकाग्रचेतसा ॥

तत्र tatra [ind.] *in or to that place, there; in that, therein, in that case, then, therefore* आस्थितः āsthitaḥ [m. nom. sg. ā-sthita] *staying on, dwelling on, abiding; one who has undertaken, performed* महात्मा mahātmā [m. nom. sg. mahā-ātman] *great soul; having a great or noble nature; Great Soul of the Universe; the Supreme Spirit* असौ asau [m. loc. sg. asu] *in the breath, life; in the vital airs or breaths of the body* योगिभिः yogibhiḥ [m. inst. pl. yogin] *by the yogis, with Strivers for Oneness* तु tu [ind.] *but, and, then, now; often an expletive* प्रगीयते pragīyate [3rd sg. pr. pass. pra-√gai] *it is praised, is celibrated* सुगीतम् sugītam [n. nom. sg. su-gīta] *well praised in songs, well sung or chanted; good singing, good song* चैव caiva [ind. ca-eva] *and even, as well as; a mere expletive* कर्तव्यम् kartavyam [n. nom. sg. kartavya: fpp. √kṛ] *to be done or made or accomplished; that which ought to be done, duty, obligation, task* मनः manaḥ [n. nom. sg. manas] *mind (in the widest sense), will, breath, thought, imagination* एक eka [mfn.] *one, that one only, single* अग्र agra [n.] *foremost point or part, tip, point* एकाग्र ekāgra [adj.] *one-pointed, fixing one's attention upon one point or object; intent, absorbed in* चेतसा cetasā [n. inst. sg. cetas] *with or by the mind*

Abiding in that place is the breath of the Supreme Spirit praised by the Strivers for Oneness. Singing well is even a duty with the mind focused on one point.

GS28 śivo binduḥ śivo devo ghargharāmṛtavarcasā | nikhilaṃ pūrayed dehaṃ viṣadāhajvarāpaham ||	शिवो बिन्दुः शिवो देवो घर्घरामृतवर्चसा । निखिलं पूरयेद्देहं विषदाहज्वरापहम् ॥

शिवः śivaḥ [m. nom. sg. śiva] *auspicious, gracious, favourable, benign, kind, benevolent; "The Auspicious One", Shiva* बिन्दुः binduḥ [m. nom. sg. bindu] *drop, globule, dot, spot; dot over a letter (the anusvāra connected with Shiva); considered as the point at which creation begins* शिवः śiva [m. nom. sg. śiva] *Shiva* देवः devaḥ [m. nom. sg. deva] *heavenly, divine; a deity, god* घर्घर ghargharа [m.] *uttered with an indistinct gurgling or purring sound; sounded like gurgling* अमृत amṛta [mfn.] *imperishable, not dead, immortal; (m.) an immortal, a god; (n.) collective body of immortals, world of immortality, heaven, eternity, immortality; nectar (conferring immortality, produced at the churning of the ocean)* वर्चसा varcasā [n. inst. sg. varcas] *with or by vital power, vigour, energy, activity, (esp.) the illuminating power of fire or the sun i.e., brilliance, light, lustre* निखिलम् nikhilam [m. acc. sg. ni-khila] *complete, all, whole, entire* पूरयेत् pūrayet [3rd sg. caus. pr. opt. act. √pṝ] *let him, it or he, it should cherish, nourish, bring up; grant abundantly, fulfill (a wish or hope), fill* देहम् deham [m. acc. sg. deha] *the body* विष viṣa [m.] *a servant, attendant; poisonous; a mystical name of the sound m* दाह dāha [m.] *burning, combustion, conflagration, heat; glowing, redness* ज्वर jvara [m.] *fever, pain, grief, sorrow; fever of the soul, mental pain* अपहम् apaham [m. acc. sg. apaha] *(ifc.) keeping back, repelling, removing, destroying*

The divine Shiva's initial manifestation, the purring imperishable sound with vital power, let the burning sound m remove sorrow and nourish the whole body.

GS29 sarpavatkuṭilākārasu- ṣumṇāveṣṭitāṃ tanum | makāraveṣṭitāṃ kṛtvā mātṛvat pariyojayet ||	सर्पवत्कुटिलाकारसु - षुम्णावेष्टितां तनुम् । मकारवेष्टितां कृत्वा मातृवत्परियोजयेत् ॥

सर्प sarpa [m.] *a snake, serpent, serpent-demon, tortuous motion* वत् vat *an affix added to words to imply likeness or resemblance; citation form of suffix vant forming possessive adjectives* कुटिल kuṭila [mf(ā)n] *bent, curved, crooked, round, running in curved lines, crisped, curled* कार kāra [mfīn] *making, doing, working, a maker, doer; the term used in designating a letter or sound or indeclinable word* अकार akāra [m.] *the letter or sound Aa, sounding Aa (the first vowel)* आकार ākāra [m.] *form, figure, shape, stature, appearance, external gesture or aspect of the body, expression of the face* सुषुम्णा suṣumṇā [f. nom. sg. suṣumṇa] *very gratious or kind; central or middle channel for vital spirit* वेष्टिताम् veṣṭitāṃ [f. acc. sg. veṣṭita] *enveloped, enclosed, surrounded; covered; twisted (as a rope)* तनुम् tanum [m. acc. sg. tanu] *thin, slender, little, minute, delicate, fine* मकार makāra [m.] *the letter or sound Ma, sounding Ma (the last stop of the consonants)* वेष्टिताम् veṣṭitāṃ [f. acc. sg. veṣṭita] *enveloped, surrounded, twisted (as a rope)* कृत्वा kṛtvā [ind.] *having done, acting, having acted, made, making, thinking of, having thought of* मातृवत् mātṛvat [ind.] *like (towards) a mother; having a mother (might refer to mātṛkā: an alphabet, the totality of letters; mother; that which comes from the mother)* परि pari *prefix expressing around, fully, abundantly, richly (esp.ibc., to express fulness or high degree), beyond, more than, "secondary"* योजयेत् yojayet [3rd sg. caus. pr. opt. act. √yuj] *one should yoke, join, fasten, unite, connect; one should concentrate (mind, thoughts)*

The shape of the twisted thin central channel for the vital spirit is like a coiled snake. Like a mother, one should unite in making the twisted sound Ma.

GS30 tristhānaṃ ca trimātraṃ ca tribrahma ca trirakṣaram | ardhamātraṃ ca yo vetti sa bhaved vedapāragaḥ ||	त्रिस्थानं च त्रिमात्रं च त्रिब्रह्म च त्रिरक्षरम्। अर्धमात्रं च यो वेत्ति स भवेद् वेदपारगः॥

त्रिस्थानम् tristhānam [n. nom. sg. tri-sthāna] *having three dwellings; extending through the three worlds* च ca [ind.] *and, both, likewise* त्रिमात्रम् trimātram [n. nom. sg. tri-mātra] *three measures of any kind; the whole of three; being nothing but three; three in number* च ca [ind.] *and, both, likewise* त्रिब्रह्म tribrahma [n. nom. sg. tri-brahman] *Brahma, Vishnu, and Shiva* च ca [ind.] *and, both, likewise; [ca ... ca] though ... yet* त्रिस् tris [ind.] *thrice, three times* त्रिरक्षरम् trirakṣaram [n. acc. sg. tris-akṣara] *consisting of three sounds* अर्ध ardha [n.] *side, part, place, region, country; "one part of two," partly, the half; (in cpd) the half part of anything* मात्रम् mātram [n. acc. sg. mātra] *(ifc.) measure, quantity, sum, size, duration, measure of any kind; being nothing but, simply or merely; having the measure of* च ca [ind.] *and, both, likewise* यः yaḥ [m. nom. sg. yad] *who, what, which* वेत्ति vetti [3rd sg. pr. indic. act. √vid] *he knows* सः saḥ [m. nom. sg. pron. tad] *he* भवेत् bhavet [3rd sg. pr. opt. act. √bhū] *he should be or become* वेद veda [m.] *knowledge, true or sacred knowledge* पारगः pāragaḥ [m. nom. sg. pāra-ga] *one who has gone through or accomplished or mastered, knowing thoroughly, profoundly learned*

Extending through the three worlds and being three in number, Brahman, Vishnu, and Shiva consist of three sounds, and he who knows half of such measures, he should become profoundly learned in sacred knowledge.

GS31 sarvataḥpāṇipādaṃ tat	सर्वत:पाणिपादं तत्
sarvatokṣiśiromukham |	सर्वतोक्षिशिरोमुखम् ।
nirmalaṃ vimalākāraṃ	निर्मलं विमलाकारं
śuddhasphaṭikasaṃnibham ||	शुद्धस्फटिकसंनिभम् ॥

सर्वत: sarvataḥ [m. nom. sg. sarvatas] *from all sides, everywhere* पाणि pāṇi [m.] *the hand* पादम् pādam [m. acc. sg. pāda] *the foot* तत् tat [ind.] *then, at that time, in that case* सर्वतोक्षिशिरोमुखम् sarvatokṣiśiromukham [m. acc. sg. sarvatas-akṣi-śiraḥ-mukham] *having eyes, head and mouth everywhere* निर्मलम् nirmalam [m. acc. sg. nir-mala] *spotless, shining, clean, pure, bright* विमला vimalā [f.] *stainless, spotless, bright, pure* आकारम् ākāram [m. acc. sg. ā-kāra] *form, figure, shape, stature, appearance, external gesture or aspect of the body, expression of the face* शुद्ध śuddha [adj.] *clean, clear, white; faultless, correct; genuine* स्फटिक sphaṭika [m.] *crystal, quartz* संनिभम् saṃnibham [m. acc. sg. saṃnibha] *like, similar, resembling; (ifc.) often pleonastically with names of colours*

Then with hands and feet everywhere, eyes, head and mouth everywhere, he is a bright stainless figure like pure clear crystal.

GS32 arjuna uvāca |	अर्जुन उवाच ।
jīvo jīvati jīvena	जीवो जीवति जीवेन
nāsti jīvam ajīvitam |	नास्ति जीवमजीवितम् ।
nirgataḥ saha saṅgena	निर्गतः सह सङ्गेन
sa jīvaḥ kena jīvati ||	स जीवः केन जीवति॥

अर्जुनः arjunaḥ [m. nom. sg. arjuna] *Arjuna* उवाच uvāca [3rd sg. perf. act. √vac] *he spoke, said* जीवः jīvaḥ [m. nom. sg. jīva] *living, existing, any living being; the principle of life, vital breath; the living or personal soul* जीवति jīvati [3rd sg. pr. indic. act. √jīv] *he lives, he remains alive* जीवेन jīvena [m. inst. sg. jīva] *by the principle of life, vital breath* नास्ति nāsti [ind. na-asti] *it is not, there is not* जीवम् jīvam [m. acc. sg. jīva] *principle of life, vital breath; any living being, anything living; life, existence* अजीवितम् ajīvitam [n. nom. sg. a-jīvita] *non-existence, death* निर्गतः nirgataḥ [m. nom. sg. nirgata] *gone out, come forth; appeared, become visible* सह saha [ind.] *together, with, along, conjointly* सङ्गेन saṅgena [n. inst. sg. saṅga] *by attachment to; by selfish attachment or affection; by sticking, clinging to* सः saḥ [m. nom. sg. pron. tad] *he* जीवः jīvaḥ [m. nom. pl. jīva] *living, existing, any living being; the principle of life, vital breath; the living or personal soul* केन kena [n. inst. sg. ka] *by what?* जीवति jīvati [3rd sg. pr. indic. act. √jīv] *he lives, he remains alive*

Arjuna spoke:
A being lives by the vital breath. There is no vital breath in death. He who is living comes with attachment. By what is it that he lives?

GS33 śrībhagavān uvāca |	श्रीभगवानुवाच।
mukhanāsikayor madhye	मुखनासिकयोर्मध्ये
prāṇaḥ saṃcarate sadā |	प्राणः संचरते सदा।
ākāśaṃ pibate nityaṃ	आकाशं पिबते नित्यं
sa jīvas tena jīvati ||	स जीवस्तेन जीवति॥

श्रीभगवान् śrībhagavān [m. nom. sg. bhagavat] *the holy or revered one; the blessed Lord, an epithet of Krishna* उवाच uvāca [3rd sg. perf. act. √vac] *he spoke, said* मुख mukha [n.] *the mouth, face, countenance; the beak of a bird* मुखनासिकयोः mukhanāsikayoḥ [n. gen. du. mukhanāsika] *of the mouth and nose* मध्ये madhye [ind.] *in the middle, midst, within, between; among, in the presence of* प्राणः prāṇaḥ [m. nom. sg. prāṇa] *the breath of life, spirit, respiration; vitality, vital energy, a vital organ* संचरते saṃcarate [3rd sg. pr. indic. mid. sam-√car] *to come near, approach, appear; to go and wander about, to go in or through, enter, traverse, pervade* सदा sadā [ind.] *always, ever, continually* आकाशं ākāśam [n. acc. sg. ākāśa] *light, clearness; free or open space, ether; the subtle fluid (supposed to fill and pervade the universe and to be the peculiar vehicle of life and sound* पिबते pibate [3rd sg. pr. mid. √pā] *he drinks, swallows; draws in, sucks* नित्यम् nityam [m. acc. sg. nitya] *everlasting, continual, perpetual, constant* सः saḥ [m. nom. sg. pron. tad] *he* जीवः jīvaḥ [m. nom. sg. jīva] *living, existing, any living being; the principle of life, vital breath; the living or personal soul* तेन tena [n. inst. sg. tad] *by that, which* जीवति jīvati [3rd sg. pr. indic. act. √jīv] *he lives, he remains alive*

Krishna spoke:
The vital breath continually enters in the middle of the mouth and nose. He who is living draws in the subtle fluid constantly, by which he lives.

GS34 kākīmukhaṃ kakārāntaṃ makāraṃ cetanānugam | akārasya tu luptasya ko 'rthaḥ saṃpratipadyate ||	काकीमुखम् ककारान्तं मकारं चेतनानुगम्। अकारस्य तु लुप्तस्य को ऽर्थः संप्रतिपद्यते॥

काकी kākī [f.] *a female crow* मुखम् mukham [n. nom. sg. mukha] *the mouth, face, countenance; the beak of a bird; the chief, principal, best (ifc.: having anyone or anything as chief); introduction, beginning, (ifc.: beginning with* ककार kakāra [m.] *the letter or sound Ka, sounding Ka (the first consonant and the first plosive or stop sound)* अन्तम् antam [m. acc. sg. anta] *a final syllable, ending, end; (ind.ifc.: as far as* मकारम् makāram [m. acc. sg. makāra] *the letter or sound Ma, sounding Ma (the last of the consonant stop sounds)* चेतन cetana [m.] *visible, excellent; conscious, intelligent; an intelligent being, man* अनुगम् anugam [n. nom. sg. anu-ga] *going after, following, corresponding with, adapted to; (ifc.) followed by* अकारस्य akārasya [m. gen.abs. sg. akāra] *of the letter or sound Aa, of sounding Aa (the first vowel)* तु tu [ind.] *but, and, then, now; often an expletive* लुप्तस्य luptasya [m. gen.abs. sg. lupta] *of dropped, lost, annihilated* कः kaḥ [m. nom. sg. ka] *the sound Ka (the first consonant)* अर्थः arthaḥ [m. nom. sg. artha] *motive, cause; sense, meaning* संप्रतिपद्यते saṃpratipadyate [3rd sg. pr. indic. pass. sam-prati-√pad] *is arrived at, attained, found*

From a female crow ending the sound of Ka up to a man sounding Ma, the meaning of Ka is found while dropping the sound a.

GS35 tāvat paśyet khagākāraṃ	तावत्पश्येत्खगाकारं
khakāraṃ tu vicintayet |	खकारं तु विचिन्तयेत्।
khamadhye kuru cātmānam	खमध्ये कुरु चात्मानम्
ātmamadhyaṃ ca khaṃ kuru ||	आत्ममध्यं च खं कुरु॥

तावत् tāvat [n. nom. sg. tāvat] *so great, so large, so much, so far, so long, so many; indeed, truly; (ind.) to such an extent, in such a number, so much, so far, so greatly* पश्येत् paśyet [3rd sg. pr. opt. act. √dṛś] *he should see, regard, consider, understand, learn, see with the mind* खग khaga [m.] *moving in the air, a bird* आकारम् ākāram [m. acc. sg. ā-kāra] *form, figure, shape, stature, appearance, external gesture or aspect of the body, expression of the face* ख kha [n.] *a cavity, aperture; the letter Kha; an aperture of the human body (the nine openings of the body: the mouth, two ears, two eyes, two nostrils, the organ of excretion and of generation); vacuity, empty space, void, air, ether, sky* कारम् कार kāra [m.n. acc. sg. kāra] *making, doing, working, forming, a maker, doer; act, action, the term used in designating a letter or sound or indeclinable word; a song or hymn of praise; a battle song* तु tu [ind.] *but, and, then, now; often an expletive* विचिन्तयेत् vicintayet [3rd sg. pr. opt. act. vi-√cint] *he should think (about), have a thought or idea, reflect (upon)* ख kha [n.] *vacuity, empty space, void, air, ether, sky* मध्ये madhye [ind.] *in the middle, midst, within, between; among, in the presence of* खमध्ये khamadhye [m. loc. sg. kha-madhya] *in the middle void, the midst of the air, between; in the space between* कुरु kuru [2nd sg. pr. imperv. act. √kṛ] *you cause!, you make!, you use!* च ca [ind.] *and, both, likewise* आत्मानम् ātmānam [m. acc. sg. ātman] *the self, oneself* आत्म ātma [in cpd for ātman] *self, own, own's own* मध्यम् madhyam [m. acc. sg. madhya] *middle, (ind.ifc.) into the midst of, into, among* च ca [ind.] *and, both, likewise* खम् kham [m. acc. sg. kha] *vacuity, empty space, void, air, ether, sky* कुरु kuru [2nd sg. pr. imperv. act. √kṛ] *you cause!, you make!, you use!, you think of!*

Truly one should see the appearance of the bird, then reflect upon a song of praise of empty space. Within empty space use the self, and within the self use empty space!

GS36 khamadhye ca praveṣṭavyaṃ khaṃ ca brahma sanātanam | ātmānaṃ khamayaṃ kṛtvā na kiṃcid api cintayet ||	खमध्ये च प्रवेष्टव्यं खं च ब्रह्म सनातनम् । आत्मानं खमयं कृत्वा न किंचिदपि चिन्तयेत् ॥

ख kha [n.] *a cavity, aperture; the letter Kha; an aperture of the human body (the nine openings of the body: the mouth, two ears, two eyes, two nostrils, the organ of excretion and of generation); vacuity, empty space, void, air, ether, sky* मध्ये madhye [ind.] *in the middle, midst, within, between; among, in the presence of* च ca [ind.] *and, both, likewise, as well as* प्रवेष्टव्यम् praveṣṭavyam [n. nom. sg. praveṣṭavya] *to be entered or penetrated or pervaded, accessible, open; one should enter or penetrate into* खम् kham [m. acc. sg. kha] *vacuity, empty space, void, air, ether, sky* च ca [ind.] *and, both, likewise* ब्रह्म brahma [n. acc. sg. brahman] *Brahman, Impersonal Expansion* सनातनम् sanātanam [n. acc. sg. sanātana] *eternal, perpetual, permanent, everlasting, ancient* आत्मानम् ātmānam [m. acc. sg. ātman] *the self, oneself* खम् kham [m. acc. sg. kha] *void, vacuum, ether; heaven; hole, exit* अयम् ayam [m. nom. sg. idam; ifc. acc. aya] *this; going* कृत्वा kṛtvā [ind.] *having done, acting, having acted, thinking of, having thought of* न na [ind.] *not, no, nor, neither* किंचिद् kiṃcid [ind.] *somewhat, a little* न किंचिद् na kiṃcid [ind.] *not somewhat, not a little; a lot, highly, intensely, particularly* अपि api [adv.] *and, moreover, also, besides, even* चिन्तयेत् cintayet [3rd sg. pr. opt. act. √cint] *one should think (about), have a thought or idea, reflect upon*

Empty space and everlasting Brahman are to be entered within empty space, and one should intensely reflect upon having used this empty space and the self.

GS37	ūrdhvaśūnyam adhaḥśūnyaṃ madhyeśūnyaṃ nirāmayam | triśūnyaṃ yo 'bhijānāti sa bhavet kulanandanaḥ ||	ऊर्ध्वशून्यमधःशून्यं मध्येशून्यं निरामयम् । त्रिशून्यं यो ऽभिजानाति स भवेत्कुलनन्दनः ॥

ऊर्ध्व ūrdhva [mfn.] *rising or tending upwards, raised, elevated, high, above* शून्य śūnya [n.] *empty, void, hollow, deserted; absent, absentminded; having no certain object or aim, distracted; possessing nothing; wholly alone or solitairy; a void, vacuum; vacuity, emptiness, nonentity* अधस् adhas [ind.] *below, down, in the lower region, beneath, under* शून्यम् śūnyam [n. nom. sg. śūnya] *void, vacuum, emptiness* मध्ये madhye [ind.] *in the middle, midst, within, between; among, in the presence of* शून्यम् śūnyam [n. nom. sg. śūnya] *vacuum, void, emptiness* निरामयम् nirāmayam [n. nom. sg. nir-āmaya] *free from illness, health; causing health, wholesome; infallible, secure* त्रि tri [m.] *three* शून्यम् śūnyam [n. nom. sg. śūnya] *void, vacuum, emptiness* यः yaḥ [m. nom. sg. yad] *who, what, which* अभिजानाति abhijānāti [3rd sg. pr. indic. act. abhi-√jñā] *he/she knows understands, is aware of, apprehends* सः saḥ [m. nom. sg. pron. tad] *he* भवेत् bhavet [3rd sg. pr. opt. act. √bhū] *he should or would be* कुल kula [n.] *a herd, troop, flock, multitude, number; a race, family, community, tribe, caste, company; the residence of a family; a house, abode; a noble or eminent family or race* नन्दनः nandanaḥ [m. nom. sg. nandana] *rejoicing, gladdening*

The emptiness above, the emptiness below, and the emptiness in the middle are infallible. Whoever is aware of the threefold emptiness, he would be gladdening a community.

GS38 tasya bhāvasya bhāvātmā	तस्य भावस्य भावात्मा
bhāvanā naiva yujyate |	भावना नैव युज्यते।
anāvṛttasya śabdasya	अनावृत्तस्य शब्दस्य
tasya śabdasya yo gatiḥ ||	तस्य शब्दस्य यो गतिः॥

तस्य tasya [n. gen. sg. pron. tad] *of him, his, for him, of this, its* भावस्य bhāvasya [m. gen. sg. bhāva] *of becoming, being; existence has* भाव bhāva [m.] *that which is or exist, being or living creature; becoming, existing; the seat of the feelings or affections, heart, soul, mind; appearance; continuance; state, true condition or state, truth, reality* आत्मा ātmā [m. nom. sg. ātman] *the self, the individual soul, (ifc.) often having the meaning of "nature of"* भावना bhāvanā [f. nom. sg. bhāvana] *the act of producing or effecting, forming in the mind, conception, thought, imagination; causing to be* न na [ind.] *not, no* एव eva [ind.] *just, as well as, even, a mere expletive* युज्यते yujyate [3rd sg. pr. indic. pass. √yuj] *is endowed with, used, united, yoked; he falls to the lot of, belongs to or suits any one* अनावृत्तस्य anāvṛttasya [m. gen. sg. an-āvṛtta] *of not turned about or round; of not retreating or frequented or approached; of not chosen; of not addressing a prayer or song to a god* शब्दस्य śabdasya [n. gen. sg. śabda] *of a name, sound, tone, voice; of oral tradition, verbal authority* तस्य tasya [n. gen. sg. pron. tad] *of him, his, for him, of this* शब्दस्य śabdasya [n. gen. sg. śabda] *of a name, of sound, tone, voice* यः yaḥ [m. nom. sg. yad] *who, what, which, that* गतिः gatiḥ [m. nom. sg. gati] *going, going away, moving, motion in general; metempsychosis, the course of the soul through many forms of life; course progress, movement; state, condition*

This existence has the nature of a being and is not even yoked with the act of being. Whoever is moving, his voice is not addressing a prayer of the oral tradition.

GS39 tatpadaṃ viditaṃ yena	तत्पदं विदितं येन
sa yogī chinnasaṃśayaḥ |	स योगी छिन्नसंशयः।
puṇyapāpaharāś caiva	पुण्यपापहराश् चैव
ye cānye pañcadaivatāḥ ||	ये चान्ये पञ्चदैवताः॥

तत् tat [n. acc. sg. pron. tad] THAT पदम् padam [n. acc. sg. pada] *footing, standpoint; position, rank, station, site, abode, home; a sign, token, characteristic* विदितम् viditam [n. acc. sg. ppp. √vid] *known, understood, learnt, perceived, known as* येन yena [ind.] *by whom or by which, by means of which, by which way; because, since, as* सः saḥ [m. nom. sg. pron. tad] *he* योगी yogī [m. nom. sg. yogin] *a yogi, a Striver for Oneness* छिन्न chinna [ppp. √chid] *cut, cut off, cut away, cut through, divided; taken away or out of; interrupted, not contiguous, disturbed; destroyed, annihilated* संशयः saṃśayaḥ [m. nom. sg. saṃ'saya] *uncertainty, hesitation, doubt in or of* पुण्य puṇya [mfn.] *auspicious, propitious, good, right, virtuous, pure, holy, sacred* पाप pāpa [m.] *a wicked man, villain;* [n.] *bad, vicious, evil, vile low; sin, vice, crime* हराः harāḥ [f. acc. pl. hara] *taking away, destroying, removing* चैव caiva [ind. ca-eva] *and even, as well as; a mere expletive* ये ye [m. nom. pl. yad] *who, which, those, those who* च ca [ind.] *and, both, likewise* अन्ये anye [m. nom. pl. anya] *others, different; other than, opposed to; another, one of a number* पञ्च pañca [in cpd for pañcan] *five* दैवताः daivatāḥ [f. acc. pl. daivata] *gods, deities* पञ्चदैवत pañcadaivata [mfn. pañca-daivata] *having five deities (organs of sense)*

The abode of THAT *is known as he is a Striver for Oneness taking away uncertainty, and is virtuous in removing sins, even those different from the five deities.*

GS40 jīvinaḥ saha gacchanti	जीविनः सह गच्छन्ति
yāvat tattvaṃ na vindati |	यावत्तत्त्वं न विन्दति ।
pāpaṃ dahati jñānāgniḥ	पापं दहति ज्ञानाग्निः
puṇyena somasūryayoḥ ||	पुण्येन सोमसूर्ययोः ॥

जीविनः jīvinaḥ [m. nom. pl. jīvin] *living beings* सह saha [ind.] *together, with, along, conjointly* गच्छन्ति gacchanti [3rd pl. pr. indic. act. √gam] *they go, move, go away, set out, come* यावत् yāvat [ind.] *as greatly as, as far as, whenever* तत्त्वम् tattvam [n. nom. sg. tat-tva] *truth, true states, realities* न na [ind.] *not, no, nor, neither* विन्दति vindati [3rd sg. pr. indic. act. √vid] *one finds, obtains* पापम् pāpam [n. acc. sg. pāpa] *bad, vicious, wicked, evil, vile* दहति dahati [3rd sg. pr. indic. act. √dah] *it burns, it consumes by fire* ज्ञानाग्निः jñānāgniḥ [m. nom. sg. jñāna-agni] *the fire of knowledge, distinction between good and bad* पुण्येन puṇyena [m. inst. sg. puṇya] *by or with auspicious, propitious, good, right, virtuous, pure, holy, sacred* सोम soma [m.] *juice, extract, esp., the juice of the Soma plant* सूर्ययोः sūryayoḥ [n. gen. du. sūrya] *of the sun*

Living beings come together whenever one does not find truth. The fire of knowledge burns away evil with the pure juice of the Soma plant and the Sun.

GS41 puṇyapāpavinirmuktir eṣa yogo ’bhidhīyate | dhṛtirodhi manodhīti saṃtoṣaṃ samidhāmṛtam ||	पुण्यपापविनिर्मुक्तिर् एष योगो ऽभिधीयते । धृतिरोधि मनोधीति संतोषं समिधामृतम् ॥

पुण्य puṇya [mfn.] *auspicious, propitious, good, right, virtuous, pure, holy, sacred* पाप pāpa [n.] *bad, vicious, wicked, evil, vile* विनिर्मुक्तिः vinirmuktiḥ [f. nom. sg. vi-nir-mukti] *liberation, freedom of or from, a release* एषः eṣaḥ [m. nom. sg. etad] *this* योगः yogaḥ [m. nom. sg. yoga] *employment, use, application, performance, yoga, Striving for Oneness* अभिधीयते abhidhīyate [3rd sg. pr. indic. pass. abhi-√dhā] *to be named or called* धृति dhṛti [f.] *holding, seizing, keeping, supporting* रोधि rodhi [n. nom. sg. rodhin] *stopping, restraining, disturbing, blocking; obstructing, overpowering or drowning (one sound by another), filling, covering* मनो mano [in cpd for manas] *mind (in the widest sense), will, breath, thought, imagination* धी dhī [f.] *understanding, intelligence, wisdom, knowledge, art, science* इति iti [ind.] *in this manner, thus, marks a quotation* संतोषम् saṃtoṣam [m. acc. sg. sam-toṣa] *satisfaction, contentedness with; content* समिधा samidhā [f.] *an oblation to fuel or firewood* अमृतम् amṛtam [n. nom. sg. amṛta] *an immortal, a god*

Liberation from good and evil, this is called Striving for Oneness. "Supporting, restraining, and wisdom of the mind" is the satisfaction of a firewood oblation to an immortal.

GS42 indriyāṇi paśuṃ kṛtvā
yo yajeta sa dīkṣitaḥ |
paraṃ brahmādhigacchanti
śabdabrahmavicintanāt ||

इन्द्रियाणि पशुं कृत्वा
यो यजेत स दीक्षितः।
परं ब्रह्माधिगच्छन्ति
शब्दब्रह्मविचिन्तनात्॥

इन्द्रियाणि indriyāṇi [n. acc. pl. indriyā] *faculties of sense, senses, sense organs* पशुम् paśum [m. acc. sg. paśu] *a domestic or sacrificial animal* कृत्वा kṛtvā [ind.] *having done, acting, having acted, prepared* यः yaḥ [m. nom. sg. yad] *who, what, which, that* यजेत yajeta [3rd sg. pr. opt. mid. √yaj] *he should sacrifice, offer, honour* सः saḥ [m. nom. sg. pron. tad] *he* दीक्षितः dīkṣitaḥ [m. nom. sg. dīkṣita] *consecrated, initiated into; prepared, ready for; priest engaged in the Dīkṣā ceremony* परम् param [n. acc. sg. para] *highest, supreme* ब्रह्म brahma [in cpd for brahman] *Brahman, Impersonal Expansion* अधिगच्छन्ति adhigacchanti [3rd pl. pr. indic. act. adhi-√gam] *they go up to, approach, accomplish; they study, read* शब्दब्रह्म śabdabrahma [n. acc. sg. śabda-brahma] *the Veda considered as the revealed sound or word and indentified with the Supreme; Vedic recitation* विचिन्तनात् vicintanāt [n. abl. sg. vi-cintana] *from or through thinking, thought*

He is the ceremonial priest who should sacrifice after preparing the sense organs of a sacrificial animal. Through the thought of a Vedic-revealed word, they go up to the supreme Brahman.

GS43 sakale dṛṣṭapāro 'pi	सकले दृष्टपारो ऽपि
bhāvaṃ yuñjati yuñjati |	भावं युञ्जति युञ्जति ।
niṣkale darśanaṃ nāsti	निष्कले दर्शनं नास्ति
svabhāvo bhāvaṃ yuñjati ||	स्वभावो भावं युञ्जति ॥

सकले sakale [n. loc. sg. sa-kala] *in all, whole; in everything, the whole (m.) in everybody* दृष्ट dṛṣṭa [ppp. √dṛś] *settled, acknowledged, decided, fixed, valid; perceived, decided, fixed; seen, understood, known, experienced* पारः pāraḥ [m. nom. sg. pāra; in cpd vṛiddhi form of para] *bringing across, the utmost reach or fullest extent; the other side, opposite* अपि api [adv.] *and, moreover, also, besides, even* भावम् bhāvam [m. acc. sg. bhāva] *that which is or exist, being; becoming, existing* युञ्जति yuñjati [3rd sg. pr. indic. act. √yuj] *it unites, joins, brings together* युञ्जति yuñjati [duplication expresses emphasis and completion or refer to two items] निष्कले niṣkale [n. loc. sg. niṣ-kala] *in without parts, undivided; in diminished, decayed; in nothing, (m.) in nobody (opposite of niṣkale)* दर्शनम् darśanam [n. nom. sg. darśana] *seeing, observing; the becoming visible or known, presence; understanding; doctrine, view, opinion* नास्ति nāsti [ind. na-asti] *it is not, there is not* स्वभावः svabhāvaḥ [m. nom. sg. svabhāva] *one's own nature, inherent-self-nature* भावम् bhāvam [m. acc. sg. bhāva] *that which is or exist, being; becoming, existing* युञ्जति yuñjati *it unites*

Besides, in everything, known and unknown unite that which is. In nothing, there is not a doctrine that one's inherent-self-nature unites that which is.

GS44 tālumūle ca lampāyāṃ trikūṭaṃ tripathāntaram | ekaṃ tattvaṃ vijānīyād vighnasyāyatanaṃ mahat ||	तालुमूले च लम्पायां त्रिकूटं त्रिपथान्तरम्। एकं तत्त्वं विजानीयाद् विघ्नस्यायतनं महत्॥

तालुमूले tālumūle [n. loc. sg. tālu-mūla] *in the root of the palate* च ca [ind.] *and, both, likewise, as well as* लम्पायाम् lampāyām [f. loc. sg. lampā] *in Lampā (name of a town and of a kingdom)* त्रिकूटम् trikūṭam [n. acc. sg. trikūṭa] *having three peaks or humps or elevations; three summits, ridges* त्रिपथ tripatha [m.n.] *reached by three roads* अन्तरम् antaram [m.n. acc. sg. antara] *(ifc.) different, other, another* एकम् ekam [m. acc. sg. eka] *one, single; unique, single of its kind* तत्त्वम् tattvam [n. acc. sg. tat-tva] *truth, true states, realities* विजानीयात् vijānīyāt [3rd sg. pr. opt. act. vi-√jñā] *one should know, understand, perceive, have knowledge of, become acquainted with* विघ्नस्य vighnasya [n. gen. sg. vighna] *of an obstacle, impediment, hindrance, opposition, any difficulty or trouble; difficulty has …(gen. form is used to translate the verb "have")* आयतनम् āyatanam [n. acc. sg. ā-yatana] *resting-place, support, seat, place, home, house, abode; an altar; a sanctuary; the place of the sacred fire* महत् mahat [n. acc. sg. mahat] *great (in space, time, quantity or degree)*

In the root of the palate and in Lampa are the three ridges reached by three different roads. One should know the single truth that opposition has great support.

GS45 chinnamūlasya vṛkṣasya	छिन्नमूलस्य वृक्षस्य
yathā janma na vidyate |	यथा जन्म न विद्यते।
jñānadagdhaśarīrasya	ज्ञानदग्धशरीरस्य
punardeho na vidyate ||	पुनर्देहो न विद्यते॥

छिन्न chinna [ppp. √chid] *cut, cut away, cut through* मूलस्य mūlasya [m. gen. sg. mūla] *of a root; basis, foundation* वृक्षस्य vṛkṣasya [m. gen. sg. vṛkṣa] *of a tree, the trunk of a tree* यथा yathā [ind.] *in which manner or way, as, like; so that* जन्म janma [m. acc. sg. janman] *the birth, life* न na [ind.] *not* विद्यते vidyate [3rd sg. pr. indic. pass. √vid] *it is found, there is* ज्ञान jñāna [n. from jñā] *knowing, knowledge* दग्ध dagdha [ppp. √dah] *burned, consumed by fire* शरीरस्य śarīrasya [n. gen. sg. śarīra] *of the body, the bodily frame* पुनर् punar [ind.] *repeatedly, again and again, again* देहः dehaḥ [m. nom. sg. deha] *the body, embodiment* न na [ind.] *not* विद्यते vidyate [3rd sg. pr. indic. pass. √vid] *it is found, there is*

Cut away the root of a tree so that there is no life; there is no re-embodiment of a body known as having been consumed by fire.

GS46 gītāḥ sugītāḥ kartavyāḥ	गीताः सुगीताः कर्तव्याः
kim anyaiḥ śāstrasaṃgrahaiḥ |	किमन्यैः शास्त्रसंग्रहैः ।
yāḥ purā padmanābhasya	याः पुरा पद्मनाभस्य
mukhapadmād viniḥsṛtāḥ ||	मुखपद्माद्विनिःसृताः ॥

गीताः gītāḥ [f. nom. pl. gītā] *songs, sacred songs* सु su [ind.] *prefix expressing well, good, excellent, right, beautiful* सुगीताः sugītāḥ [f. nom. pl. sugītā] *excellent songs or sacred songs* कर्तव्याः kartavyāḥ [f. nom. pl. kartavya] *to be done or made or accomplished or executed; that which ought to be done, duties, obligations* किम् kim [ind.] *what?, how?, whence?, why?* अन्यैः anyaiḥ [n. inst. pl. anya] *by others, different; by other than, opposed to; by or with another* शास्त्र śāstra [n.] *any book or treatise; any manual; any sacred book* संग्रहैः saṃgrahaiḥ [m. inst. pl. saṃgraha] *by or with collections* याः yāḥ [f. acc. pl. yad] *who, what, which, that* पुराः purāḥ [f. acc. pl. purā] *before, formerly, of old; hitherto, up to the present time, until now* पद्मनाभस्य padmanābhasya [m. gen. sg. padmanābha] *of the "lotus-naveled", name of Vishnu* मुखपद्मात् mukhapadmāt [m. abl. sg. mukha-padma] *from a "lotus-face"* विनिःसृताः viniḥsṛtāḥ [m. nom. pl. vi-niḥsṛta] *gone forth or out, issued forth, sprang from*

Songs, beautiful sacred songs, are to be performed, and whence for other collections of sacred books? What sprang from Vishnu's "lotus-face" until now?

GS47 gītāgāṅgodakaṃ pītvā	गीतागाङ्गोदकं पीत्वा
punarjanma na vidyate |	पुनर्जन्म न विद्यते।
sarvaśāstramayī gītā	सर्वशास्त्रमयी गीता
sarvadharmamayo hariḥ ||	सर्वधर्ममयो हरिः॥

गीता gītā [f.] *song, sacred song or poem* गाङ्गः gāṅgaḥ [m. nom. sg. gāṅga] *being in or on the Ganges, coming from or belonging or relating to the Ganges* दकम् dakam [n. nom. sg. daka] *water* पीत्वा pītvā [ind.] *having drunk or quaffed; after drinking* पुनर् punar [ind.] *repeatedly, again and again, again* जन्म janma [m. acc. sg. janman] *the birth, life* न na [ind.] *not* विद्यते vidyate [3rd sg. pr. indic. pass. √vid] *it is found, there is* सर्व sarva [n.] *whole, entire, all, everything* शास्त्र śāstra [n.] *any book or treatise; any manual; any sacred book* मयी mayī [f. nom. sg. mayī] *(ifc.) made or formed or produced from or consisting of or compared to* गीता gītā [f. nom. sg. gītā] *song, sacred song or poem* सर्व sarva [m.n.] *whole, entire, all, everything* धर्ममयः dharmamayaḥ [m. nom. sg. dharma-maya] *consisting of virtue, moral, duty, righteous* हरिः hariḥ [m.f. nom. sg. hari] *carrying, having, bearing; a horse, a lion; epithet of Vishnu-Krishna, Shiva, etc.*

There is no re-birth after drinking the water of the Gita and the Ganges. Of all the sacred books produced, the Gita is the most virtuous.

GS48 sarvatīrthamayī gaṅgā	सर्वतीर्थमयी गङ्गा
sarvapāpakṣayaṃkarī |	सर्वपापक्षयंकरी ।
sarvabhogamayaś cāyaṃ	सर्वभोगमयश्चायं
sarvamokṣamayo hy ayam ||	सर्वमोक्षमयो ह्ययम् ॥

सर्व sarva [m.n.] *whole, entire, all, everything* तीर्थ tīrtha [n.] *a passage, way, road, stairs for landing or for descent into a river, bathing-place, place of pilgrimage on the banks of sacred streams, piece of water* मयी mayī [f. nom. sg. mayī] *(ifc.) made or formed or produced from or consisting of or compared to; containing* गङ्गा gaṅgā [f. nom. sg. gaṅgā] *the river Ganges* सर्व sarva [m.n.] *whole, entire, all, everything* पाप pāpa [n.] *bad, vicious, wicked, evil, vile* क्षयंकरी kṣayaṃkarī [f. nom. sg. kṣayaṃkara] *(ifc.) causing destruction or ruin* सर्व sarva [m.n.] *whole, entire, all, everything* भोग bhoga m. *enjoyment, eating; profit, utility, pleasure, delight* मयः mayaḥ [m. nom. sg. maya] *(ifc.) made or formed or produced from or consisting of or compared to* च ca [ind.] *and* अयम् ayam [m. nom. sg. idam] *this one, this, that* सर्व sarva [m.n.] *whole, entire, all, everything* मोक्ष mokṣa [m.] *release from worldly existence or transmigration, final or eternal emancipation; liberation* मयः mayaḥ [m. nom. sg. maya] *(ifc.) made or formed of or produced from or consisting of or compared to; containing* हि hi [ind.] *for, because, on account of; certainly; a mere expletive* अयम् ayam [m. nom. sg. idam] *this one, this, that*

Containing all the places of pilgrimage on the banks of sacred streams, the Ganges is causing destruction of all evil, and this is full of delight because it contains the release from all worldly existence.

GS49 gītā gaṅgā ca gāyatrī	गीता गङ्गा च गायत्री
govindo hṛdi saṃsthitāḥ |	गोविन्दो हृदि संस्थिताः ।
caturgakārasmaraṇāt	चतुर्गकारस्मरणात्
punarjanma na vidyate ||	पुनर्जन्म न विद्यते॥

गीता gītā [f. nom. sg. gītā] *song, sacred song or poem* गङ्गा gāṅgā [f. nom. sg. gāṅga] *being in or on the Ganges, coming from or belonging or relating to the Ganges* च ca [ind.] *and, both, likewise, as well as* गायत्री gāyatrī [f. nom. sg. gāyatrī] *any hymn composed in the ancient meter of 24 syllables, often a triplet of eight syllables each* गोविन्दः govindaḥ [m. nom. sg. govinda] *(lit.) "ox-finding," name of Krishna* हृदि hṛdi [n. loc. sg. hṛd] *in the heart, soul, mind* संस्थिताः saṃsthitāḥ [m. nom. pl. saṃ-sthita] *standing; placed, resting, lying, sitting; abiding, remaining* चतुर् catur [m.] *four* गकार gakāra [m.] *the letter or sound Ga, sounding Ga* स्मरणात् smaraṇāt [n. abl. sg. smaraṇa] *from the act of remembering or calling to mind; from being mentioned in Smṛti* पुनर् punar [ind.] *repeatedly, again and again, again* जन्म janma [m. acc. sg. janman] *the birth, life* न na [ind.] *not* विद्यते vidyate [3rd sg. pr. indic. pass. √vid] *it is found, there is*

The Gita, the Ganges, and the sacred Gayatri hymn abide in the heart of Krishna. There is no re-birth after sounding the four Ga[s] from memory.

GS50 gītāsāraṃ paṭhed yas tu hy acyutasya ca saṃnidhau | tasmād guṇasahasreṇa viṣṇor nirvacanaṃ yathā ||	गीतासारं पठेद्यस्तु ह्य् अच्युतस्य च संनिधौ। तस्माद्गुणसहस्रेण विष्णोर्निर्वचनं यथा॥

गीता gītā [f.] *song, sacred song or poem* सारम् sāram [n. acc. sg. sāra] *the core or pith or solid interior of anything; firmness, strength power, energy; the substance or essence or heart or essential part of anything, best part, quintessence; (ifc.) "chiefly consisting of or depending on"; a compendium, summary (often in titles of books)* पठेत् paṭhet [3rd sg. pr. opt. act. √paṭh] *he should read or repeat aloud, recite, rehearse; peruse, study; teach, cite, quote, mention, declare* यः yaḥ [m. nom. sg. yad] *who, what, which, that* तु tu [ind.] *but, and, then, now; often an expletive* हि hi [ind.] *for, because; certainly; a mere expletive* अच्युतस्य acyutasya [m.n. gen. sg. a-cyuta] *of firm, solid; of imperishable, permanent; of Krishna or Vishnu* च ca [ind.] *and, both, likewise, as well as* संनिधौ saṃnidhau [m. loc. sg. sam-ni-√dhi] *in juxtaposition, nearness, vicinity, presence* तस्मात् tasmāt [ind.] *from that, therefore, than that, on that account; thus* गुण guṇa [m.] *quality, Basic Attribute* सहस्रेण sahasreṇa [n. inst. sg. sahasra] *by or with thousand* विष्णोः viṣṇoḥ [m. gen. sg. viṣṇu] *of Vishnu* निर्वचनम् nirvacanam [m. acc. sg. nir-vaca] *not speaking, silent, blameless; (ind.) silently*; [n. nom. sg. nir-vaca] *speaking out, pronouncing; a saying or proverb; interpretation, explanation, etymology* यथा yathā [ind.] *in which manner or way, as, like; so that; according to what is right, properly*

Now he who is in the presence of Vishnu should recite the Gitasara, thus with a thousand Basic Attributes of Vishnu, an explanation according to what is right.

GS51 etat puṇyaṃ pāpaharaṃ
dhanyaṃ duḥsvapnanāśanam |
paṭhatāṃ śṛṇvatāṃ caiva
viṣṇor māhātmyam uttamam ||

एतत्पुण्यं पापहरं
धन्यं दुःस्वप्ननाशनम् ।
पठतां शृण्वतां चैव
विष्णोर्माहात्म्यमुत्तमम् ॥

एतत् etat [n. nom. sg. etad] *this, this here, here* पुण्यम् puṇyam [n. nom. sg. puṇya] *auspicious, propitious, good, right, virtuous, pure, holy, sacred* पापहरम् pāpaharam [n. nom. sg. pāpa-hara] *removing or destroying evil* धन्यम् dhanyam [n. nom. sg. dhanya] *bringing or bestowing wealth, opulent, rich; fortunate, happy, auspicious* दुःस्वप्ननाशनम् duḥsvapnanā-śanam [n. nom. sg. duḥ-svapna-nāśana] *removing bad dreams* पठताम् paṭhatām [3rd sg. pr. imperv. mid. √paṭh] *one must or has to read or repeat aloud, recite, rehearse; peruse, study; teach, cite, quote, mention, declare* शृण्वताम् śṛṇvatām [3rd pl. pr. imperv. mid. √śru] *men or people must or have to hear, listen or attend to anything; have to hear or learn anything about; have to hear (from a teacher), study, learn* चैव caiva [ind. ca-eva] *and even, as well as; a mere expletive* विष्णोः viṣṇoḥ [m. gen. sg. viṣṇu] *of Vishnu* माहात्म्यम् māhātmyam [m. acc. sg. māhātmya] *magnanimity, highmindedness; exalted state or position, majesty, dignity* उत्तमम् uttamam [m. acc. sg. ud-tama] *uppermost, highest, chief; most elevated*

This is sacred, is destroying evil, is bringing wealth, is removing bad dreams. One has to recite and many have to learn about the exalted state of Vishnu!

iti śrīmahābhārate bhiṣmaparvaṇi gītāsāraḥ samāptaḥ ||
इति श्रीमहाभारते भिष्मपर्वणि गीतासारः समाप्तः ॥
Thus ended the Gītāsāra in the Bhiṣmaparvan in the sacred Mahābhārata.

Kashmiri Gītāsāra

In English

Gītāsāra

1–2. *Arjuna spoke:*
As for this world here below nothing is Brahman, gone beyond the spotless heaven, an entire undisturbed perfect isolation (*Kavailya*), genuine, perpetual, virtuous, unimaginable, unintelligible, annihilation without coming into existence. O Krishna, liberated by Striving for Oneness by knowledge, speak about the knowledge of THAT!

3. *Krishna spoke:*
Light in the sky everywhere, all beings endowed with the Basic Attributes everywhere, the highest self everywhere, I resided in a superior abode.

4. The eternal divine great light is beyond the enduring sound, beyond the superior abode, beginning with a sound without Basic Attributes.

5. Coming to THAT, the ultimate light, is through the ultimate enduring sound state. From an era within the four-age cycle up to this day, it has not been told to anyone.

6. The embodied self is created by Me as well as the Primordial Substance and the field. Everything should become the field; nothing is the superior abode.

7. O Arjuna, they hear with clarity from you, the best of sages! Now they are liberated, O Mighty Armed One, due to clarity from you, O Winner of Wealth.

8. There is no application of the right perception of sacred knowledge, of truth, of focus on the beginnings of the Samkhya philosophy by all the heretics together.

9. Besides, the knowledge of the gods told by Me is difficult to find. The divine universal form is developed by the dot knot related to Bhairava.

10. The central subtle channel on the southern path is understood by its universal nature. As for this secret question, your discourse is with Me.

11. Not fire, air and ether, not earth or even water, not mind, intelligence or self-consciousness is the secret motive of your discourse.

12. One goes to incidental continuance when one does not see that which exists. Ether is sounding pure Aa, the enduring sound of imperishable bliss.

13. Evidently without Basic Attributes, mankind continues entirely as before. The supreme intelligence of Brahman is perhaps all that is, and of this [mankind] is not aware.

14. The relation of the three worlds and Krishna is without persevering effort, having been reached through the measure of a finger's breadth for the tenth time and staying in internal space.

15. After having disappeared when the living soul returned to this prescribed whole, the moving and unmoving are now pervaded by the three worlds.

16. To be meditated upon THAT with THAT is knowledge indeed. Then they respect THAT beginnings, known by Brahman and illuminated in the complete knowledge of the Vedas.

17. They say: "The sacred knowledge in the Vedas" is the abode of true knowledge and the supreme thought of whoever has understood the supreme THAT. He is a sage who has mastered true knowledge.

18. This offering is the highest to be known, and is an established religious act. This is the supreme, most famous Gayatri hymn named Hamsa, the vehicle of Brahman.

19. Certainly, religious austerity is thus when the Veda is honored by the sages. Whoever understands this small part, he is called one who is learned of a small part.

20. Those knowing who is released by a life from childhood to old age are men with thorough knowledge. Many are released by knowing the faults that cause one to fall.

21. The left channel for the vital spirit is like the divine river Ganges, the right channel for the vital spirit is like the river Yamuna, but between these two is the third, and one should remember that place of sacrifice.

22. The left channel for the vital spirit is indeed related to Vishnu's subtle channel, the right channel to Brahman's subtle channel, and the middle channel is the subtle channel for the female energies of the deities. The three, carrying the breath of life, call to mind Brahman, Vishnu, and Shiva, and the three breath exercises, recaka, pura, and kumbhaka.

23. Whoever is aware of division is going in the middle. He is a powerful Striver for Oneness, always fixed upon one subject and resorts to the knowledge of Brahman.

24. Truly, the left channel for the vital spirit and the western fire of the altar, the right channel for the vital spirit and the eastern fire of the altar, the middle channel for the vital spirit and the southern fire of the altar, prescribed the three sacred fires.

25. He stands firmly within the light and the Soma circle. The Soma circle is in the middle, and in the midst thereof is the disk of the Sun.

26. The disk of the sun is between the glow of the flames and the offering of food. In the middle of the food offered is light from smokeless charcoal.

27. Abiding in that place is the breath of the Supreme Spirit praised by the Strivers for Oneness. Singing well is even a duty with the mind focused on one point.

28. The divine Shiva's initial manifestation, the purring imperishable sound with vital power, let the burning sound *m* remove sorrow and nourish the whole body.

29. The shape of the twisted thin central channel for the vital spirit is like a coiled snake. Like a mother, one should unite in making the twisted sound Ma.

30. Extending through the three worlds and being three in number, Brahman, Vishnu, and Shiva consist of three sounds, and he who knows half of such measures, he should become profoundly learned in sacred knowledge.

31. Then with hands and feet everywhere, eyes, head and mouth everywhere, he is a bright stainless figure like pure clear crystal.

32. *Arjuna spoke:*
A being lives by the vital breath. There is no vital breath in death. He who is living comes with attachment. By what is it that he lives?

33. *Krishna spoke:*
The vital breath continually enters in the middle of the mouth and nose. He who is living draws in the subtle fluid constantly, by which he lives.

34. From a female crow ending the sound of Ka up to a man sounding Ma, the meaning of Ka is found while dropping the sound *a*.

35. Truly one should see the appearance of the bird, then reflect upon a song of praise of empty space. Within empty space use the self, and within the self use empty space!

36. Empty space and everlasting Brahman are to be entered within empty space, and one should intensely reflect upon having used this empty space and the self.

37. The emptiness above, the emptiness below, and the emptiness in the middle are infallible. Whoever is aware of the threefold emptiness, he would be gladdening a community.

38. This existence has the nature of a being and is not even yoked with the act of being. Whoever is moving, his voice is not addressing a prayer of the oral tradition.

39. The abode of THAT is known as he is a Striver for Oneness taking away uncertainty, and is virtuous in removing sins, even those different from the five deities.

40. Living beings come together whenever one does not find truth. The fire of knowledge burns away evil with the pure juice of the Soma plant and the Sun.

41. Liberation from good and evil, this is called Striving for Oneness. "Supporting, restraining, and wisdom of the mind" is the satisfaction of a firewood oblation to an immortal.

42. He is the ceremonial priest who should sacrifice after preparing the sense organs of a sacrificial animal. Through the thought of a Vedic-revealed word, they go up to the supreme Brahman.

43. Besides, in everything, known and unknown unite that which is. In nothing, there is not a docrine that one's inherent-self-nature unites that which is.

44. In the root of the palate and in Lampa are the three ridges reached by three different roads. One should know the single truth that opposition has great support.

45. Cut away the root of a tree so that there is no life; there is no re-embodiment of a body known as having been consumed by fire.

46. Songs, beautiful sacred songs, are to be performed, and whence for other collections of sacred books? What sprang from Vishnu's "lotus-face" until now?

47. There is no re-birth after drinking the water of the Gita and the Ganges. Of all the sacred books produced, the Gita is the most virtuous.

48. Containing all the places of pilgrimage on the banks of sacred streams, the Ganges is causing destruction of all evil, and this is full of delight, because it contains the release from all worldly existence.

49. The Gita, the Ganges, and the sacred Gayatri hymn abide in the heart of Krishna. There is no re-birth after sounding the four Ga[s] from memory.

50. Now he who is in the presence of Vishnu should recite the *Gita-sara*, thus with a thousand Basic Attributes of Vishnu, an explanation according to what is right.

51. This is sacred, is destroying evil, is bringing wealth, is removing bad dreams. One has to recite and many have to learn about the exalted state of Vishnu!

Thus ends the *Gītāsāra* in the *Bhiṣmaparvan* in the sacred *Mahābhārata.*

Note added April 16, 2019.

In Wiig 1981, pp. 66 and 158, the *Gītāsāra* is mentioned as the other title of the *Oṃkāra-Māhātmya*, assigned to the Skanda-Purāṇa literature. There is no translation of this work nor of the Kashmiri *Gītāsāra* mentioned in Appendix E, p. 167–176. I am grateful to Alexandra van der Geer for this reference and her search for a translation of the Kashmiri *Gītāsāra*. I thank also Chris Chapple and David Gordon White for informing me that they have not seen a translation.

Bibliography

Bagchee, Joydeep and Vishwa Adluri, "Who's Zoomin' Who? Bhagavadgītā Recensions in India and Germany," *International Journal of Dharma Studies*, 2016, Vol. 4:4, pp. 1–41.

Bedekar, V. M., Review of "Shri Bhagavad Gītā (Bhojapatri with Complete 745 Verses)," (7th Edition) by Acharya Shri Charanatirth Maharaja, *Annals of the Bhandarkar Oriental Research Institute*, 1964, Vol. 45, pp. 161–163.

Belvalkar, S. K., "The Bhagavadgītā "Riddle" Unriddled," *Annals of the Bhandarkar Oriental Research Institute*, 1939, Vol. 19, pp. 335–348.

——, *The Bhagavadgītā. Being reprint of relevant parts of Bhīṣmaparvan* from B.O.R. Institute's edition of the *Mahābhārata* for the first time critically edited, Poona, 2nd reprint, 1968.

Bhattacharjya, Sunil Kumar, *The Original Bhagavad Gita Complete with 745 Verses (including all the Rare Verses)*, Parimal Publications, 2014.

Kuiken, Gerard D. C., *Svābhāvikasūtra, The Roots of the Bhagavadgītā*, Vol. II, OTAM Books, The Hague, 2018, reprint 2023.

——, *Svābhāvikasūtra, The Roots of the Bhagavadgītā*, Vol. III, OTAM Books, The Hague, 2018, reprint 2023.

——, *Dating the Bhagavadgītā, a Review of the Search for Its Original, and the Class-Caste System with Its Generic Evidence*, uploaded on www.ResearchGate.net and www.Academia.edu, October 2016.

Rastogi, Navjivan, "Contribution of Kashmir to Philosophy, Thought and Culture," *Annals of the Bhandarkar Oriental Research Institute*, 1975, Vol. 56, pp. 27–43.

Saha, Nirinjan, "*Bhagavadgītā*: A Bird's Eye View of Its Historical Background, Formation, and Teaching," *Journal of Indian Council of Philosophical Research*, 2018, Vol. 35, pp. 139–157.

Wiig, Linda,"Māhātmyas: A Preliminary Descriptive Survey (Including a List of Māhātmyas Compiled From Aufrecht's Catalogus Catalogorum)" (1981). Theses (South Asia Studies).

www.ingramcontent.com/pod-product-compliance
Ingram Content Group UK Ltd.
Pitfield, Milton Keynes, MK11 3LW, UK
UKHW041919190726
13854UKWH00003B/1328

9 789078 623151